LANDSCAPING
from the Ground Up

LANDSCAPING
from the Ground Up

Sara Jane von Trapp

The Taunton Press

Taunton
BOOKS & VIDEOS

for fellow enthusiasts

First printing: 1997
Printed in the United States of America

The Taunton Press, Inc., 63 South Main Street,
PO Box 5506, Newtown, CT 06470-5506
e-mail: tp@taunton.com

Library of Congress Cataloging-in-Publication Data

von Trapp, Sara Jane.
    Landscaping from the ground up / Sara Jane von Trapp.
      p.   cm.
    Includes index.
    ISBN 1-56158-185-2
    1. Landscape gardening.   2. Landscape architecture
    I. Title.
SB473.V67   1997
712'.6 — dc21   97-6978
                                      CIP

To my mother and father,
whom I love dearly,
and who have never let me down

Acknowledgments

I want to give special thanks to my children, Kate, Jakob, and Rebecca, for their strength, maturity, and clarity about life despite their tender ages. I learn from you every day, and you are more precious to me than you know.

Thank you to T, without whom this book would not have been written. Thump, thump, thump.

I would like to say thank you to a few people at The Taunton Press: to Helen Albert for giving me this opportunity; to Cherilyn DeVries for her patience and understanding throughout this process; and to Tom Johnson for the use of his yard, shown in some of the photos.

Many thanks to Barry Estabrook and Regula Noetzli for technical wisdom. For allowing us access to job sites and for giving us permission to photograph their work, kudos to Joseph Scott, Ralph Malanca, and Don Bashak of Glen Gate Company in Wilton, Connecticut, and to Bob Bociek and his crew of Laflamme Services, Inc., in Bridgeport, Connecticut. Thanks to Tim and Mary Volk for many kindnesses, but most recently, for allowing me to include their patio in this book.

Others who offered assistance and materials along the way were Dave Negri and Ed Sakl of Tilcon Connecticut, Inc., Anthony Nazzaro of Bethel Sand and Gravel Co. in Bethel, Connecticut, and Lexington Gardens in Newtown, Connecticut.

Contents

Introduction

No matter the size of the challenge, I never tire of gardening and creating new landscapes—it replenishes my spirit. I am sure I am not alone in my reveling. Millions of people across the United States are awakening to the thrill of gardening and are hungry for the knowledge and expertise needed to fulfill their fantasy landscapes.

For the last 20 years I have been helping homeowners realize their landscaping goals. Now it's your turn to realize the potential of your landscape. Perhaps you are having a home built or are living in a new home, and you have a barren lot in desperate need of a makeover. Or maybe you have a tired, overgrown yard that's begging for a face-lift.

This book can help you change your situation for the better. In it I will explain how to develop a landscape that works well with your neighborhood and with the architecture of your home—one that combines both function and form to create a yard that reflects the personality and lifestyle of you and your family. This is not an easy job. It will take time, patience, and oftentimes muscle. But all your efforts will be reflected in the beauty of the landscape.

To achieve a successful landscape makeover, it is essential to have a well-developed plan divided into steps and performed in logical order. I will show you how to create an efficient and economical plan that, even if phased in over a period of years, will harmonize when the job is completed.

You'll also learn how to assess and adjust the grade of your site and how and when to perform a soil test. You'll see how to integrate yard structures such as retaining walls, walkways, patios, fences, and shade structures into the landscape and how to design and build them to last.

I'll show you how to start a lawn from scratch and how to design planting beds that blend color, texture, shape, and size to create year-round interest in the yard. I'll also give you a few ideas on how to jazz up the yard with specialty gardens, such as rock gardens and water gardens.

You can create the yard of your dreams with imagination and good planning. I hope this book provides you with enough information about tools, technique, and theory that you have the confidence to build your own landscape from the ground up.

How to Use This Book

I recommend using this book as you would a cookbook. Just as a chef would take a recipe from a book and add his own twists, experienced gardeners will be familiar with basic gardening techniques, and so they will take the subjects from within these pages and add their own flavor and ideas. Inexperienced gardeners, on the other hand, will use this book as a starting point to gather more information about the techniques.

Both the seasoned and novice gardener will find the Sources and Further Reading sections very useful. Sources will guide you to companies that sell plant seeds and bulbs, garden tools and equipment, materials for retaining walls and patios, fences, and garden structures. Further Reading provides a list of books that can give you more information about specific subjects within each chapter, such as building water gardens or decks.

Also in the back of the book is the USDA Plant-Hardiness Zone Map, which will help you pick plants that are appropriate for your climate. This map will be a great help to anyone drawing up a landscape plan.

Although most gardeners will find this book useful for its strategic approach to various landscape techniques, such as installing a patio or drawing a landscape plan, some of these techniques will be beyond the reach of the novice gardener. What I have done is lay out the basic steps in the process so that anyone can understand what is involved. This will help you evaluate costs and work effectively with a contractor or landscape professional. This information will also help you make informed decisions about the landscape design and how its elements should be built.

For those wanting to hire a professional to do the job, I will tell you where you can save money by splitting tasks or by offering assistance. For example, many homeowners hire a contractor to do the rough grading of the landscape, but they'll do all the finish grading themselves. Doing so can save significant money, which can be spent on plants. I'll also give some common-sense guidelines to hiring and working with a landscape architect, designer, or contractor.

CHAPTER 1
Making the Grade

Every landscaping project begins at ground level. The existing land must first have the proper grade to achieve successful results. Grade is simply the degree of inclination of a land area. It determines which direction water will flow through the yard and how fast. A ditch or valley will harbor or catch water, a slope will move water, and level ground will cause water to stand still until it is absorbed by the soil, provided the soil drains well.

Because grade determines the direction and speed of water flow in your yard, it will largely influence your landscape design. For instance, standing water may well mean certain death for shrubs or trees in a planting bed and could also become a breeding area for mosquitoes or other insects. A patio or walkway must shed water to avoid puddling and ice, which will eventually cause cracks in the stone or concrete. Moisture near the house foundation may cause mildew and deterioration of siding, or even the foundation. Any of these factors could necessitate regrading of the yard.

If you are constructing an outbuilding, a pool, or other structure, like an addition to your house, regrading to change the direction of water flow also is necessary. But redirection of water flow may not be the only instances where regrading is necessary. For example, ditches and hummocks in the lawn area are not only difficult to mow and dangerous to traverse, but if severe, they can be unsightly. To remedy this situation, you may want to level these areas or make the slopes less severe.

In this chapter I'll illustrate the importance of grade and its relation to your landscape plan. I'll also show you how to determine the grade of your yard and offer a few suggestions on how to fix it, if needed. I'll also illustrate how to deal with sloped sites. But before I show you how to change the grade, let's take a look at how the grade has taken shape.

HOW SETTLING AFFECTS GRADE

The grade of any yard is subject to the whims of nature. It can be altered by tree roots, rocks, or even burrowing animals. All of these things will ultimately redirect water flow and thus will influence your yard. However, grade is most affected by settling, which occurs after new construction or after a new excavation. Air pockets left in the soil gradually work their way out, causing the soil level to drop. Settling occurs all over the yard, and it's the amount of compaction that dictates how much settling will occur.

If your site was graded and compacted carefully, resulting in a positive grade, regrading to correct water flow will be minimized. A positive grade is achieved by sloping the land away from the foundation, allowing water to flow away from the house (see the drawing below). To minimize settling, the soil should be carefully compacted with a flat-headed hand tamper or with a plate compactor, a motor-driven walk-behind machine that mechanically tamps the soil.

If you have water leaking into your basement, it might be because your yard has a negative grade, in which the land slopes toward the

POSITIVE GRADE

A positive grade is established when the soil is highest at the foundation and slopes away from the house.

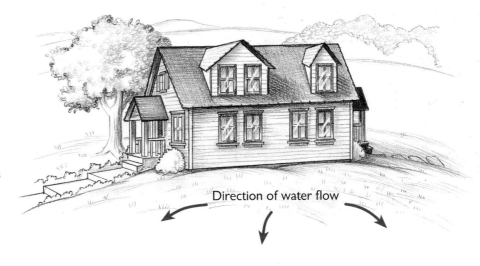

Direction of water flow

NEGATIVE GRADE

When the soil is graded so that the low point is at the foundation, it is called negative grade.

Direction of water flow

SETTLED SOIL

It is obvious that an electrical line was buried on the property because the soil on the excavation has settled, resulting in a depression from the street to the meter base on the house. Additional soil is necessary to fill the depression and to disguise the excavation.

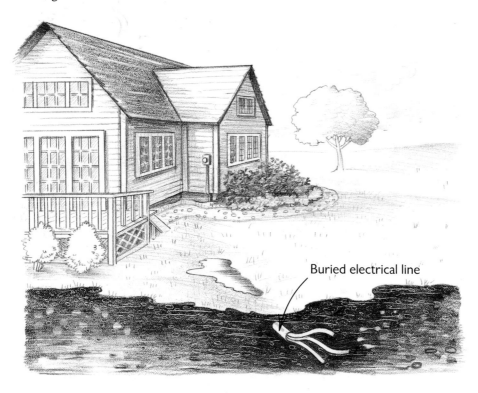

Buried electrical line

foundation (see the top drawing at left). Water flows toward the foundation from the yard, slides down the wall, finds a flaw in the concrete or block, and then flows inside. Patching the concrete won't solve the problem. But regrading the yard so that it slopes away from the foundation will help.

A negative grade can be caused simply by an existing slope in the yard, but most often it's the result of hasty excavation work around the foundation. Sometimes the backfill around the foundation is not compacted enough by the bulldozer because it is unable to get very close to the house to run over those areas. Rather than hand-tamping or using a plate compactor, the excavator loosely backfills and tamps the soil against the foundation with the bucket of the bulldozer. Over time, the soil in these areas settles and drops below the level of the surrounding yard.

Settling does not just occur around the foundation. If an underground pipe, an electric line, or a tank in a yard has been replaced, and the soil is not backfilled and compacted sufficiently, settling will occur, leaving a distinctive gully for the length of the excavation (see the bottom drawing at left). A client of mine has spent years replenishing the soil around an auxiliary septic tank installed in her yard. In her case, the right degree of compaction was difficult to achieve after the tank was installed because the excavation around this type of tank had to be carefully backfilled, or the tank could collapse. Even after careful hand-tamping, a little settling has gone on for years. This settling has eventually slowed as soil has been added and as the grade has been adjusted over time. This may seem to be a relentless, annoying job, but if my client did not maintain and adjust the grade occasionally, an unsightly and unsafe depression would result, marring the middle of her yard.

DETERMINING GRADE

In some yards, you can tell by eye whether the grade is positive or negative and where the major slopes are. But in other yards, grade may be wholly imperceptible to the eye. In either situation, you need to measure the grade to determine the degree of slope. There are two basic ways to do this: with a transit or with stakes and string. Which method you choose will largely depend on the size of your yard, but it may depend on which method you are most comfortable using.

Transit

If your yard is large (over a quarter acre), the best way to determine its grade is to use a transit (see the photo at right). You can rent a transit at a rental center for about $30 per day. The job requires two people: one to look through the transit's lens and another to hold a measuring stick at various locations in the yard.

To use a transit, first make sure it is level. Then focus it on the measuring stick, which is held at various high and low points in the yard. Start by experimenting with obvious measurements, such as the front-door threshold vs. the bottom of the steps, just to get the hang of using the tool. After a few easy measurements, sketch a map of the yard, including landmarks like

A transit can be used to determine the highs and lows of a yard. The tool requires two people: one to look through the lens and another to hold a measuring stick.

trees, the house, the garage, and plot your measurements on this map. Use the high point of the yard as your reference and subtract each measurement from that. You will quickly see a pattern and where low points will need to be regraded.

Stake-and-string method

If your yard is small, or a transit is too daunting, you can determine the grade simply by using stakes and string. Drive a stake in a low area of the yard and tie a string

around it. Pull the string taut toward the foundation or house. Use a construction level to make sure the string is level and then nail it to a high point on the foundation or house, making sure the string is still taut and level (see the photos on p. 8).

Sketch a map of your yard, including landmarks. Measure from the string to the ground at various intervals to find the low points and mark them on the map. Then pull

When determining grade with the stake-and-string method, make sure the string is level, then take the measurement at the house, continuing outward (left). The low point in this yard is measured short of the stake (above), where the grade begins to climb again.

the stake at the low point and drive it into another area in the yard. Again, make sure the string is taut and level, then take the measurements and plot them. Repeat as necessary. Subtracting the low-point measurements from the high-point measurement will show you the contour of the yard and will help you judge whether there's a negative or positive grade.

CORRECTING GRADE

Once you've determined the existing grade of your yard, you can begin correcting it, if needed. But before you go outside and begin moving earth or hire a pro to do it, it's important to have in your mind a general landscape plan.

Determine what areas of your yard will be lawn and planting beds and what areas will become walkways, decks, patios, pools, or other landscape elements. You don't need to be very specific just yet, but you must have enough of a plan that you avoid unnecessary work where a swimming pool will be excavated or where a deck or patio will be built at a future date. The plans can be fine-tuned later.

Rough grading

The first job is rough grading, which consists of regrading the yard so that water flows in the direction you want it to—most important, away from the foundation. Ideally, to move water adequately, the grade must have 1 in. of slope in 8 ft. of distance. For example, to achieve a positive

grade from the foundation, the soil level 8 ft. from the house all the way around needs to be at least 1 in. lower than at the foundation, more to be safe and to allow for settling.

If your yard is small, or if the amount of regrading is not substantial, you can rent a skid-steer loader (often called a Bobcat, after one of the manufacturers) from the local rental center and regrade the area yourself. The skid-steer loader will cost about $250 per day—it could be more or less, depending on where you live and whether you need a trailer to haul it. If you plan ahead with a neighbor, you may be able to share the cost and the machine. After regrading, the slope should be checked a couple times with a transit or with the stake-and-string method to make sure the necessary adjustments have been made.

Although a skid-steer loader is a simple machine to run, regrading takes skill and precision. So if your yard is large, or if you're not comfortable with doing the rough grading yourself, hire a landscaper or excavator. To save money, have the professional do just the rough grading, leaving the finish grading to you, which consists of smoothing the surface and sifting out the rocks from the soil.

Before digging anywhere in your yard, it's a good idea to notify the local utility companies so you can make sure there are no electrical lines or gas or water pipes in the way. The utilities will send a representative out to the site, who will locate pipes or wires and indicate how far away from them you can dig.

Spreading topsoil

Once the grade is set, topsoil will need to be spread, if you are establishing a lawn (see Chapter 9). A good lawn is best established with at least 4 in. of topsoil. If the existing soil on the property is light and relatively free of debris, it may be good enough. But if the existing soil is not acceptable—if it is gravelly, heavy (meaning it is mostly clay), or deplete of organic matter—it may be necessary to bring in topsoil from another site to augment or replace it.

The best way to determine if you need to bring in topsoil is to have a soil test done by your local university or state agricultural station. The test results will allow you to make informed decisions about what needs to be added to the existing soil or whether it needs to be replaced altogether (I'll discuss soil and soil testing in Chapter 2).

In new construction, it is not unusual for contractors to move the topsoil of your building site to another site where a lawn is being put in. Later, when your house is finished, the contractor will bring in topsoil from another site to your site. What is brought in may be perfectly good soil—but it might not be. If you're having a home built, ask that the existing soil remain on the property until you have it tested. Don't just have it respread on the site. If you do need to bring in better topsoil, you will avoid paying twice for soil to be spread.

Compacting the soil

After the topsoil has been spread, it's important to make sure that the yard is compacted sufficiently so that settling will not be a problem later on. I don't advocate running heavy machinery like a bulldozer or skid-steer loader all over the yard, especially if the soil is heavy and/or wet. Pounding the soil repeatedly with heavy machinery can alter the soil texture and damage the soil enough to make plant growth difficult and nutrient uptake impossible. But a certain amount of compaction is necessary to avoid excess settling, particularly around the foundation, under areas where you plan to build a patio or walkway, and beneath areas where retaining walls will be constructed.

Compacting the soil is best achieved by hand-tamping or with a plate compactor. There are no

These rakes are all tools used in the finish-grading process. The grading rake (the one with the wide head on the right) is used to pick out small rocks and debris. The others are used to smooth the surface.

hard-and-fast rules to judge whether the soil is compacted enough. All I can say is that it comes with experience.

Finish grading

Once the rough grading has been completed, the areas are finish-graded. The best way to do this is with a grading rake, which has a wide head with teeth that catch small rocks and debris near the surface (see the photo on p. 9). Tackle small areas, say 10 ft. by 10 ft. Drag the rake toward you, scraping only the surface to pull rocks free. Digging too deep could alter the grade you just established. If you must move large amounts of soil, use an ordinary straight rake. A leaf rake is helpful for very light scraping.

DEALING WITH SEVERELY SLOPED SITES

Correcting the grade is a relatively simple job on a site that is pretty much flat. But what if the site is severely sloped? Severe slope creates special problems for the landscaper. One of the biggest problems is that slope may carry water where you do not want it to go and could create swampy areas in the yard, usually at the base of the slope.

In this section I'll show you how to redirect water flow in a yard with a severe slope, how to ease a severe slope, and how to create a slope in a level yard—and why you'd want to.

Planning

When dealing with a severely sloped site, planning is important. One of the first things to consider is where you want excess water to

flow. On a large lot, it may not matter where the water flow is redirected because there is plenty of space for it to move through. On a small lot, however, be wary of neighboring properties, vegetation, and existing catch basins. You would not want to create a path leading to your neighbor's yard or an existing hedgerow or planting, which may result in puddling or the ultimate drowning of the plants.

Whenever possible, water should be directed toward a catch basin or a dry well. A catch basin is a receptacle that holds water runoff or drainage and directs it to a sewer system. It is typically made of concrete and has a cast-iron grate on top. Catch basins are usually located in the street, near the curb,

although they are sometimes installed within a landscape. A dry well is simply a hole in the ground filled with aggregate material like gravel or stone, which allows the water to percolate away (see the drawing on the facing page).

There are a couple methods that you can use to redirect water from a severe slope to a catch basin or dry well: create a swale or build a subsurface drainage system.

Creating a swale

I've found that the easiest method is to create a swale in the yard (see the drawing below). A swale is a very shallow channel that will carry the water to the catch basin, dry well, or existing waterway, such as a pond or stream (you may need

SWALE

A swale is a shallow trench that directs water to another location, such as a catch basin in the street.

Swale

Catch basin

permission from local and/or state authorities to direct water to an existing waterway). This technique is especially effective in a large yard because the swale is easily hidden. In general, the larger the space with which you have to work, the more invisible the swale will be.

You don't need heavy machinery to make a swale. The job simply requires a shovel and a straight rake. Simply dig a shallow channel, pitched so that water will flow where you want it to, and finish-grade the soil with the rake. Then plant grass seed.

Installing a subsurface drainage system

Although it is less expensive and more desirable to reshape the land to provide drainage and the proper grade, sometimes a subsurface drainage system is the only option for redirecting water.

A subsurface drainage system is often used when a neighbor's house is close to your property or when an obstacle like a grove of trees blocks the way. In these instances you need to move water but at the same time keep it away from the neighbor's house and the trees, all the while trying to avoid creating a swamp. A subsurface drainage system may also be employed in situations where regrading won't help: for instance, in areas where the slope is severe, where the soil is heavy (meaning it does not drain well), or where there's an underground spring on the site.

A subsurface drainage system could include installing a dry well, a catch basin, piping, or building a system that includes some or all of these components. These jobs are most often better handled by professionals. But you can save money by doing some of the easier tasks yourself, such as laying pipe, backfilling, or finish grading.

There are a few subsurface drainage systems that are effective. Which option you choose will depend on how well your soil drains.

Dry well If the soil is not too heavy, a dry well may be sufficient (see the drawing below). It is installed at the base of a severe slope. The size of the dry well will depend on the amount of water to be moved and on whether your soil drains well. The dry well is filled with gravel to within 4 in. of the surface, which will percolate the water down through the ground. Four inches of topsoil is laid on top of that, then grass seed is planted.

Dry well and drainage tiles
If your soil is not too heavy, a dry well can be installed and connected to underground drainage pipes, called tiles, which are perforated to distribute water along the run of piping (I recommend using 4-in. plastic field drainage tile).

DRY WELL

Construct a dry well at the base of a severe slope, which will draw water away from the surface.

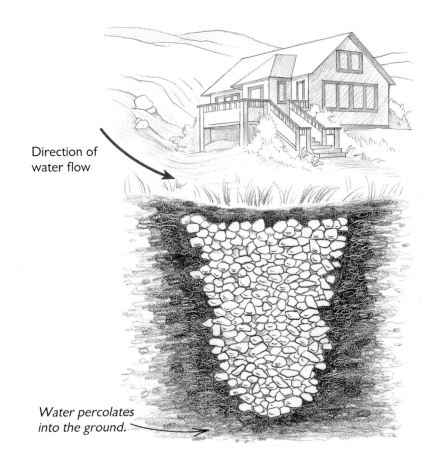

Direction of water flow

Water percolates into the ground.

DRY WELL AND DRAINAGE TILES

Drainage tiles (which are perforated) distribute water from the dry well along their run.

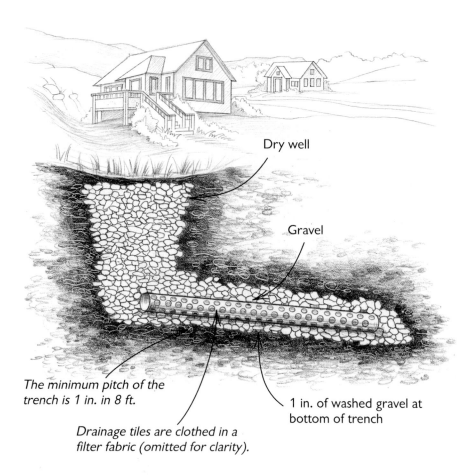

Dry well

Gravel

The minimum pitch of the trench is 1 in. in 8 ft.

1 in. of washed gravel at bottom of trench

Drainage tiles are clothed in a filter fabric (omitted for clarity).

After the dry well is installed, a trench is dug deep enough to set drainage tiles at the bottom of the dry well (see the drawing above) and long enough to reach its destination, usually another dry well, a catch basin, a pond (remember to check with the authorities about whether this is legal), or just away from the problem area (depending on the size of the lot). The depth of the trench will depend on the grade drop between the inlet and the outlet. The minimum pitch of the trench is 1 in. in 8 ft.—more to be safe, say 2 in. in 8 ft.—and it should be checked continuously during the dig.

After the trench is finished, at least 1 in. of washed gravel is added at the bottom before the drainage tiles are installed. The gravel prevents the tiles from sitting directly on the soil at the bottom of the trench and facilitates drainage. The tiles should be clothed in a plastic filter fabric, which repels soil and pebbles that will clog the openings but allows water to pass through. Once the fabric is in place, a few more inches of gravel is added, then the trench is carefully backfilled and covered with at least 4 in. of topsoil.

Dry well and solid pipe   The worst-case scenario is the need to move a lot of water without distributing it along the way, which may be the case with an underground spring, or if the soil is very heavy and therefore does not drain well. In any of these instances, a dry well is installed at the problem area, and 4-in. solid pipe (with a filter-fabric sock on the open end) is run underground from the well to another dry well or catch basin (see the drawing on the facing page). In areas with city sewer systems, the pipe can be attached directly to a catch basin if there's one nearby. Another option is to pipe the water to a pond or stream, if there's one available and if it's legal to use as a receptacle.

A trench is dug from the dry well to the destination. As before, the depth of the trench will depend on the grade drop between the inlet and the outlet. The pipe must be pitched away from the dry well (at least 1 in. in 8 ft.). If a catch basin is the destination, the pipe can connect directly to knockouts in the basin.

Holding back severe slopes

If a yard is severely sloped, water movement might not be the only consideration: aesthetics is another. I find that a graduated slope is much more attractive and offers more landscape design possibilities.

Terraces   The most graceful way to deal with slope is to create a series of terraces that graduate the slope. Each terrace can serve as a space for plantings, patios, and decks. Adding steps through the terraces make each level easily accessible (see the photo below). The stairs can be informally designed to strike a mood of meandering through the plantings, or they can have a businesslike approach, moving straight from top to bottom. Either way, the strain of climbing will be eased by the flat areas between the slopes of the terraces.

The terraces are easily shaped with a skid-steer loader and need not be straight or uniform. (If you prefer, you can hire an excavator to do the rough work, leaving the finish work to you.) In most cases, you will need excess soil with which to work, whether recycled from the slope or another area of the yard or brought in. If you don't want to employ retaining walls in the

DRY WELL AND SOLID PIPE

To move a lot of water in a soil that is heavy, dig a dry well and run 4-in. solid pipe from it to a catch basin.

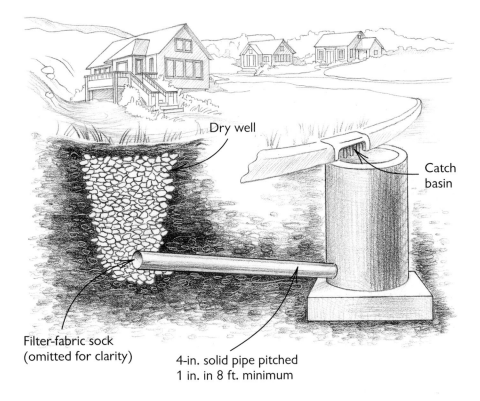

Dry well

Catch basin

Filter-fabric sock (omitted for clarity)

4-in. solid pipe pitched 1 in. in 8 ft. minimum

Steps in a terraced area make different levels readily accessible. A landing is sometimes necessary to bridge the space between steps.

SMALL-YARD RETAINING WALL

A retaining wall is an ideal method of holding back slope in a small yard.

design, the terraces must be gradual and shallow, which requires a great deal of space to distribute the slope.

Retaining walls If you don't have a lot of space to make the terracing gradual and shallow, retaining walls may be necessary (see the drawing above). Retaining walls can be built from a variety of materials: Large boulders can be used to form a rip-rap wall (see the drawing on the facing page); smaller dry-laid stone allows for serpentine or straight walls (see the drawing on p. 16); wood can be installed to form angles or a series of straight walls; concrete wall systems can also be used (retaining walls will be discussed in detail in Chapter 5). The decision on which materials to use should balance economy, ease of installation, and aesthetics.

A retaining wall can have steps through it and plants at the top, hanging down over it to make the wall less imposing. Plantings at the bottom of the wall will break up the height as well. No matter what the method or the material, weep holes (if not inherent to the structure, as in a stone wall) should

RIP-RAP TERRACING

Retain a large yard with terracing using boulders. This is called rip-rap.

be incorporated into the wall(s) for water to pass, and the area below the wall must then be treated as a separately graded space, taking all the rules of pitch and water movement into account once more.

Creating slope

Slope is not always a bad thing in a landscape. As a matter of fact, there

may be times when you would actually want to create slope in the yard. An example would be raised planting beds. The most difficult problem to address is making the higher level look natural. A former employer of mine loved mounded island plantings, but cautioned that if made too high, they looked like gravesites in high-water areas.

The best way to disguise raised soil levels is to build a retaining wall, preferably in a serpentine fashion, and to put soil behind it, making a raised bed on the back side that creates the illusion of height from the front. This differs from a free-standing wall because you are actually backfilling and planting a mounded bed that is visually two

STONE-WALL TERRACING

Dry-laid stone-wall terraces are refined but time-consuming to build.

sided, albeit giving an entirely different effect depending on which side you are standing. Both ends should gradually blend into the existing soil level.

The width of the raised bed on the back side depends on the space you have. But no matter what length or width of the raised bed, the height of the wall should be low, below 3 ft. at its highest point.

I once had a client with a perfectly flat, suburban yard who wanted to break up the front yard. Instead of building a two-sided stone wall to break up the yard, we built a short wall and backfilled to create a raised bed with a gradual slope, which added dimension and interest to an otherwise static, boring area.

CHAPTER 2
Down and Dirty

Soil Science 101 was the bane of my existence during my junior year in college. Not only was it an inherently boring course, but the class also started at 8 A.M. in a dim auditorium with comfortable, theater-type seats. The class was taught by a tyrant who delighted in singling out those who dared doze during his monologues. He was no Jay Leno, and doze I did. However, I managed to ingest enough information to realize how important soil is to plant life. From the soil, plant roots obtain nutrients, water, oxygen, and support—all that are needed for successful plant growth.

HOW A PLANT TAKES IN NUTRIENTS

A plant gets its essential nutrients from certain chemical elements, which are taken into the plant in the form of ions either through the leaves or the roots.

Hydrogen, carbon, and oxygen are taken in through the leaves.

Iron, calcium, sulfur, nitrogen, phosphorus, potassium, and trace elements are taken in through the roots.

In this chapter, I'll pass on the essentials of what I learned from that soil-science class as well as what I've learned from years of working with the soil. You'll learn about soil testing and how to use the information from that test. First, let's get down to the basics.

UNDERSTANDING SOILS

Soils are divided into groups, identified according to their makeup, which includes permeability (how well water and air move through it), texture (whether it is fine or coarse), and chemical elements. These properties, and their relationship to one another, all factor into whether your soil will successfully support plant life. A delicate balance is necessary. This information is important to understanding the results of a soil test, which I'll discuss later.

Permeability

To grow healthy plants, soil must be loose enough to allow water to penetrate but not so open as to let the water leach right through. It must hold water for roots but not to such a degree as to create a standing pool. It also must be aerated enough for roots to take in oxygen at all times but not so much that it prevents roots from continuous contact with moist soil particles.

Texture

The texture of soil is dictated by the mixture of "separates"—the solid particles that compose the soil. The three basic types of separates are sand—which is broken down into five textures: very coarse, coarse, medium, fine, and very fine—silt, and clay. Of these, sand is the largest, with silt being about 100 times smaller than sand, and clay being about 1,000 times smaller than sand.

The type of soil in your yard is determined by the relative percentages of sand, silt, and clay that are present. And there are an infinite number of possible combinations of these separates.

Understanding what type of soil you have allows you to predict many aspects of its behavior, such as how easily it can be worked and how well it will hold water and nutrients. I have seen soil so slippery, gooey, and claylike, that I could make pottery with it. I've also seen soil so sandy that the yard was like the Sahara. In general, good planting soil is somewhere between these extremes.

Chemical elements

Along with soil permeability and texture, plant growth is influenced by chemical elements. Plants receive essential nutrients from 16 chemical elements: carbon, hydrogen, oxygen, phosphorus, potassium, nitrogen, sulfur, calcium, iron, magnesium, boron, manganese, copper, zinc, molybdenum, and chlorine. Plants take in these elements in the form of ions through either their leaves or roots (see the drawing on the facing page), and a delicate balance of these elements is required to offer the best conditions for plant growth.

The amount of some elements a plant receives is dependent on the pH (the level of acidity or alkalinity) of the soil (see the graph at right). Several factors influence soil pH: the source or earthly origination of the soil, the addition of nitrogen fertilizers, rain, and the secretion of hydrogen ions by plant roots.

The level of acidity or alkalinity is measured on a scale of 1 to 14, with 7 being neutral. A pH below 7 means the soil is more acidic; a pH

EFFECT OF pH ON SOME PLANT NUTRIENTS

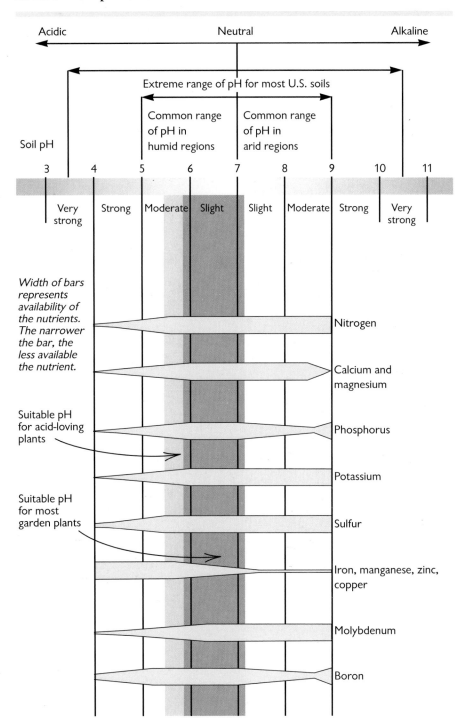

above 7 means the soil is more alkaline. In general, a pH of 6.5 to 7 is best for most plants.

Adjusting pH   If a soil is too acidic, it can cause nutrient deficiencies and toxicities. Most plants do not grow to their potential in soil that is acidic, a couple of exceptions being rhododendrons and blueberries (see the photos below).

Acidity is lessened or neutralized by adding lime to the soil. When added in the proper quantities, lime balances plant nutrients, adds calcium, and makes the essential nutrients of nitrogen, phosphorus, and potassium more available. The most common types of lime are ground limestone, ground dolomitic (high magnesium) limestone, and hydrated lime.

Knowing the soil texture is essential to adding the right quantity of lime (the soil-test results will tell you the

soil texture). For instance, if your soil is clay or if it contains a lot of organic matter, more lime is needed to change the pH than if your soil is sandy. It's also possible to add too much lime. Adding too much lime will seriously deplete certain essential nutrients, especially phosphorus, so heed the results of the soil test and follow directions carefully on how much lime to add.

If the soil has a high alkaline level, some elements that provide essential nutrients, such as

Many plants are particular about the pH of the soil in which they thrive, like these acidic soil lovers, highbush blueberry (above) and PJM rhododendron (right).

phosphorus, become unavailable to plants. To lower the pH, add sulfur to the soil, following the amount recommended by the soil-testing lab. You can buy sulfur in spray or dust form at your local garden center.

TESTING SOIL

Now that you have an understanding of basic soil science, you can take the first—and most important—step in your landscaping project: Test the soil.

Any college or university with an agriculture department can test your soil, and all states have soil-testing labs. The lab will determine what kind of soil you have, what nutrients are present and deficient, and the pH of the soil. The lab will even recommend what nutrients to add and at what rates, depending on what you want to grow. A soil test usually costs from $10 to $20, depending on where you live and how many samples you send, but it's money well spent. It will take about three weeks to get the results back. (If you're so inclined, you can buy a soil-testing kit from a garden catalog or a garden center and do the test yourself.)

If you're testing the soil for the whole yard, take samples from different parts of the yard. Use a spade or trowel and dig a few ½-in. slices of soil (see the drawing at right). Mix the slices together in a pail, and extract a small representative sample for each area and send it to the lab. Label each sample so that you'll remember where it came from. If you are interested in sampling just a small portion of the yard, say for a vegetable garden, you would still dig up several soil slices and mix them together, but dig only from that one patch of ground where the garden will be located.

To receive the most pertinent information for your circumstances, be specific about the plants you want to grow. Don't just say trees and shrubs; say roses, yews, tomatoes, or grass. The lab will tell you whether the soil is good for your planned plantings and whether you need to add certain nutrients to support them.

WORKING THE SOIL

After you've received the soil-test results, you can begin working the soil, which encompasses grading, planting, and adding nutrients. I discussed grading in the previous chapter, and I'll be more specific about planting later in the book. Right now let's talk about adding nutrients to the soil.

Adding nutrients

There are two ways to add nutrients to the soil: through organic material and through chemical fertilizers. I am not of one school or the other—as a matter of fact, I have used both. I have used rotted manure and compost for perennials and chemical fertilizers in the form of slow-release tablets for trees and shrubs. I have used organic materials on lawns for clients concerned about their children and pets playing on grass treated with chemicals.

DIGGING A SOIL SAMPLE

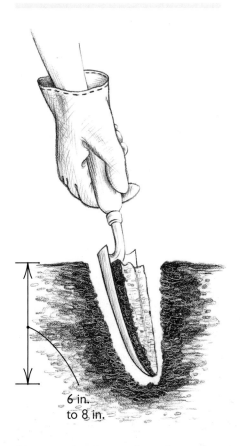

6 in. to 8 in.

Use a spade or trowel to take a ½-in. slice of soil.

SOIL-WORKING GUIDELINES

Before you grab your shovels and rakes and begin working the soil in your yard, I want to pass along a few important words of advice on how to proceed.

• Never work the soil when it's wet. You will ruin the structure. A clay soil will become an unpenetrable mass, and even the best sandy loam will become so compacted that water and air will be unable to penetrate the surface.

• Use the results of your soil test to determine which plants will do well on your property. Don't try to grow plants that are not compatible with your soil conditions. I once had a client who adored rhododendrons and azaleas, which thrive in acidic soil, and she spent a lot of money at my garden center replacing them on an annual basis. When we chatted about the situation, she said she was finally giving in to her soil. It turns out that her yard had been the site of a limestone quarry, and no amount of acid additives was going to make a difference. You cannot expect to change the soil in your entire yard without spending a fortune. Also, it's hard to tell how far down to dig out the old soil so that the plant roots won't reach it.

• It is uneconomical and almost impossible to completely change the texture of your existing soil. You'd have to add 6,000 lb. to 10,000 lb. of sand per 1,000 sq. ft. of clay soil just to adjust the top 6 in. But you can improve the water-holding capacity of your soil, its drainage, and its nutrient levels by improving the soil structure. For instance, you can add organic matter to sandy soil for better water-holding capacity, or you can add sand to clay soil to make it more workable.

• Follow the directions and warnings on any product you use, including fertilizer, lime, and pesticides. This is not a case where if a little works, more will work better. Using more than the recommended dosages may be harmful not just to plants but also to wildlife and people, as some additives leach into the water system sooner or later.

nitrogen—but it also has other benefits.

For instance, shredded bark, straw, or compost can be spread on the surface of the soil as a mulch to reduce erosion, to deter weeds, to lower soil temperature in summer or raise it in winter, and to hold in moisture around plant roots.

You can buy shredded bark and straw at your local nursery. But compost is the least-expensive way to add organic matter into the soil, because you can make it yourself in your own backyard. Composting is a great way to recycle both yard waste and kitchen waste. Food waste (except for meat products and bones), grass clippings, garden weeds, hay, tree leaves, and sawdust (except that from pressure-treated wood) are all good components of a compost pile.

The most efficient way to compost is to buy a commercial composting bin or to make one yourself. It doesn't have to be large—4 ft. by 4 ft. is probably sufficient for most small- to medium-size yards. The drawing on the facing page shows plans for a compost bin that's pretty easy to build. If you prefer, you can substitute chicken wire for the 1x slats on the sides of the bin.

To make a compost pile, alternate 6-in. layers of the waste with 2 in. of soil. Adding lime to the layers will hasten the decomposition of the waste. Turn the pile once a month with a pitchfork or shovel to make the components break down faster. Humidity is needed for composting activity, so after completing a level, make sure the top of the pile is concave to catch rainwater.

Each method has its own advantages. For instance, organic matter adds nutrients to the soil and improves its texture and water-holding capacity naturally. The drawback is that organic matter requires frequent applications. Chemical fertilizers, on the other hand, are more concentrated, so less is needed to be effective, and fewer applications are necessary. The choice of additives is yours.

Organic matter Supplementing the existing soil with organic matter is not only a good way to provide nutrition for plants—especially

As the decomposition ensues, the temperature of the pile will be as high as 150°F in the center, high enough to kill microorganisms and any diseases present in the yard waste so that they do not harm the plants later when the compost is spread. The compost pile is ready for use when all the elements have decomposed.

If you have the space (and the waste), it's a good idea to have more than one compost pile going at the same time. Keeping them all at

different stages will ensure that you always have a ready supply of mature (well-decomposed) compost.

Use only well-decomposed organic matter around your plants, whether it be compost or manure. Fresh organic matter generates high temperatures as it breaks down and robs the soil of nitrogen, which will be harmful to the plants. Noncomposted pruning debris may harbor diseases that ordinarily would be killed by the high temperatures of composting. Fresh sawdust will

cause the same problems and may even burn the ground beneath if you are not careful (fresh sawdust is perfect for annihilating weeds or grass that you want to eliminate).

Chemical fertilizers   There are no hard-and-fast rules for adding nutrients with chemical fertilizers. All plants differ in their nutritional requirements (what chemical elements are needed). Worst of all, the nutritional requirements could change as the plant's life cycle changes. The best advice I can give

A SMALL COMPOST BIN

Quantity	Description	Size
4	2x4 posts	4 ft.
1	2x4 brace	4 ft. 7 in.
2	2x4 blocks	3½ in.
33	1x4 slats	4 ft.
14	1x4 slats (for front)	3 ft. 6 in.
4	1x2s	4 ft.

MATERIALS LIST

First assemble the side panels on a flat surface. Then stand them up and nail on the back slats.

Form the groove for the front slats by nailing two 1x2s about ¾ in. apart, allowing enough room for the 1x4s to fit loosely.

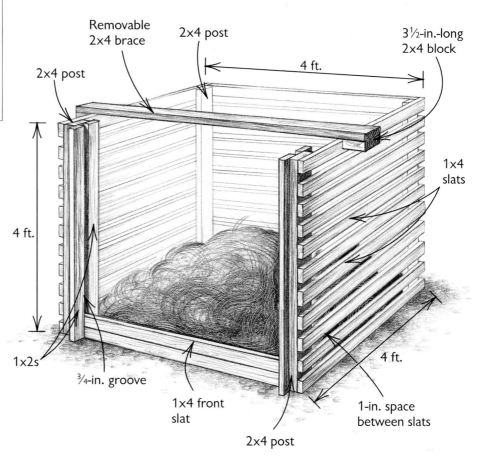

Removable 2x4 brace

2x4 post

3½-in.-long 2x4 block

2x4 post

4 ft.

4 ft.

1x4 slats

4 ft.

1x2s

¾-in. groove

1x4 front slat

2x4 post

1-in. space between slats

4 ft.

The three major components of lawn and garden fertilizer are nitrogen (N), phosphorus (P), and potassium (K). A balanced fertilizer includes all three, often in different amounts, depending on the application of the fertilizer.

is that you should follow the recommendations of the lab that performed your soil test. If you were specific about what plants you wanted to grow in the soil, the lab will tell you exactly what to add and at what rates. That's why it's important to specify what plants you plan to grow.

Chemical fertilizers generally use their element symbols to describe what is in the bag (see the photo above). Nitrogen (N), phosphorus (P), and potassium (K) are the components of most commercially produced fertilizers. A fertilizer with components of 20-11-12 means there is almost twice the amount of nitrogen as phosphorus, and half the amount of potassium as nitrogen. A fertilizer labeled 10-10-10 means there are equal parts of all three elements in the bag. It is possible to purchase simply phosphorus (0-20-0) if it is your only requirement.

Before applying a chemical fertilizer, check your town ordinances: Some towns require the homeowner to place a warning sign in the yard if chemical fertilizers have been added to the soil.

BRINGING IN NEW SOIL

If the soil test indicates that your soil is in really bad shape, you can bring in new (and hopefully better) soil from another site.

I don't recommend the wholesale exchange of soil in any yard. It is not only costly, but you also never know how deep to go when removing the existing soil. For example, in one instance, the soil in an area where a shade tree was to be planted was removed and replaced with better soil. The tree's roots loved the new soil so much that they wrapped around each other in the new soil, never extending beyond, until they girdled themselves. Ultimately, the tree died.

Hauling in topsoil to help improve the soil you have is another story. This is common to help support new lawns or vegetable gardens. If you opt to bring in new soil to your yard, it should be free of debris and weeds, and you should know the source. It should also be tested before it is brought in, so that you know what you're dealing with.

A friend of mine told me a story about some neighbors who had built a home and ordered new topsoil for the lawn area. No sooner had it arrived and been spread for seeding than a strange smell emanated from the yard. What had been passed off as clean topsoil was actually fill from an old gas station with leaky tanks. Needless to say, not only would the homeowners not want their children to play in it, but also no grass or plant would ever grow in it. It also required guys in white space suits to truck it away at exorbitant cost.

Don't assume that soil coming from a local farm is good soil. If the soil was scraped from a corn field, atrozine, a common herbicide used on corn, could be present. It remains in the soil for at least six years, and your plants will not survive it. Unfortunately, the soil test will not search for atrozine, so if you know the soil is coming from a corn field, it's probably best to avoid it altogether.

CHAPTER 3

Your Neighborhood and Your Yard

People have different reasons for landscaping their yards, whether it be for beauty or for function. But one thing homeowners often overlook is the monetary benefit of a well-landscaped yard. Statistically, landscaping adds 15% to 20% to the value of your home and helps a home sell faster. I've read many a real-estate ad that boasted of a lovely landscaped yard, a roomy deck, or a shaded nook.

If a landscape is to gain back your investment in time and money and to provide you with long-term enjoyment and satisfaction, it must be carefully planned. One of the first steps in designing a landscape involves analyzing your family's needs—both present and future—and observing your neighborhood and its overall style. Another factor is the climate in which you live.

FROM THE INSIDE OUT

How does the landscape look from your living-room window? When planning a landscape, remember that it will be seen from inside the house as well as from the outside.

INVOLVING FAMILY IN DESIGN

As a landscape designer, I realize that the home is a reflection of its owners, so I literally do my homework with them. First I spend time walking around the yard alone, visualizing how I would use the areas. Then I walk around with the homeowners and ask them how they envision the spaces. We feed ideas back and forth, talk about "what ifs," and try to learn what we can about each other's tastes. This is not only a good way to get acquainted, but it's also a wonderful way to begin generating ideas.

I also note traffic patterns around the property, from house doors, garages, and existing decks and patios. These patterns should be considered in designing the landscape, but they can be altered with careful planning.

Even without asking, I usually get a tour of the inside of the house. Once inside, I seize the opportunity to see how the landscape looks—or could look—from the inside, say from the kitchen window or from the living-room couch (see the drawing at left).

While inside, I get a feel for how the family lives. I can tell whether their lifestyle is formal or informal, and I can get a good idea of their tastes by observing how the home is decorated. I am insistent about spending time with all members of the household—including pets—to learn about their lifestyle and habits. I ask about color preferences and about plant likes and dislikes. I ask about their gardening experience and find out

what kind of garden they would like to grow, whether it's a functional vegetable garden or a decorative rock garden. I ask if they want to spend their free time taking care of the garden or if they would rather leave the maintenance to someone else.

When planning a garden, it's important to get the family involved so that everyone can enjoy the fruits of the labor. Before putting your landscaping plan on paper, interview your family, including children, to find out how they would like to use the yard. Don't ignore your pets, either, because they have habits that will impact the landscape. Also consider whether the landscape will be a place for entertaining guests. Finally, in your analysis, try to look ahead and consider the family's future plans.

Family members

If you have children, no matter what age, they will most certainly impact the landscape. So, along with conducting interviews with the adult members of the family, talk to the children in the house.

Children have special needs in a landscape. When young, they may need confined play areas, play equipment, and safe surfaces to play on. You will want the play area easily accessible and viewable from inside the house, preferably from a room in which you spend a lot of time.

As kids mature, they need more open space to play in. For instance, a confined space may later give way to a baseball diamond or a volleyball court, so trees and planting beds should be located to

CANINE ROUTE

Being a creature of habit, your dog will beat a path through a garden regardless of attempts to keep him out. Plan gardens outside of Rover's usual path.

ensure there will be room for open spaces in the future.

Pets

If you have pets that spend time in the yard, observe their habits and traffic patterns. You don't want a planting bed blocking your dog's habitual path from the house to the yard. I can't tell you how many planting beds I have shaped or moved to accommodate a pet's

habits. Some people use low mesh fencing to keep the dog out of the bed, but it's tacky to put a fence in the middle of a beautiful, new landscape (see the drawing above).

If you keep a dog or other animals in a pen, site it for convenience by making it easily accessible. But keep aesthetics in mind, too, by building the pen in a location that's not prominent. You want people to

focus on your beautiful flower beds, not on Rover's pen.

Entertaining

Many people entertain guests in the yard. If you do, think about how many people typically join you. You should consider the normal party, not the once-a-year large gathering, and plan the spaces to accommodate the average number of people you entertain.

If you're planning a patio or deck, its size will be determined by your lifestyle: Will it be an eating and cooking area, a place for sunbathing on a chaise lounge, a place for entertaining, or a nook for drinking early-morning coffee and reading the paper?

Size the patio or deck to accommodate not only people but also the furniture (see the drawing at right). Measure any furniture that will be located on it—don't forget the barbecue—and draw the pieces on your plan. Remember to leave extra space to allow chairs to be pushed away from any tables. And don't forget to allow extra space in the yard for convenient pathways around the deck or patio.

If you have a large yard, you have more flexibility to accommodate your entertaining and lifestyle needs. But if your yard is small, like in a city, economy of space is a critical issue. In a small space, design the landscape to serve multiple purposes (see the drawing on the facing page). There are a few ways you can do this. One method is to plant vegetables and flowers in containers or in small planting beds. For a small patio or deck area, build storage areas into benches or other furniture, and put wheels on furniture so that they can easily be moved around to make room for a play space.

Future plans

With your present needs figured out, look ahead. What future plans do you have for the yard? Most homeowners phase in their landscaping over time—some even take years. Planning ahead doesn't mean it's necessary to leave parts unfinished. It simply allows you to

A PATIO FOR LIVING

Plan a patio large enough for the whole family and all your furniture. Leave room for pulling out chairs and for walking around furniture.

make future plans easier and more economical to achieve, and allows the parts to be well integrated.

To make a long-term project come together effectively, it's important to consider any additions you may make to the house. Study the spots you would most likely add on to and plan the landscape around it. Don't plant a tree in that area or build a deck in the way.

Do you plan on adding any other structures to the yard, such as a swimming pool, a pond, or a storage shed? If so, don't put a patio, deck, or garden in the path of any heavy machinery you'll need to dig the pool or pond with. And don't plant any trees or flower beds in these areas.

If you don't have the money to install a patio now, but you plan to do it five years down the line, you have time to get some shade trees started so that they will be of decent size when the patio is finally built. Allow sufficient room for root and branch growth, and site the trees for optimum shade on the future patio or deck.

LOOKING AT THE NEIGHBORHOOD

After you've made a careful study of your family and its needs, it's time to take a careful look at the character of your home and your neighborhood. There are no hard-and-fast rules about keeping to the urban, suburban, or rural style of the neighborhood, but I believe

MULTIPURPOSE SPACE

In a small space, furniture can also serve as storage space. It's also a good idea to have wheels on the furniture so that it can be moved around to make room for play space.

Indigenous materials like native stone blend with the natural landscape.

Fencing should be in keeping with the architecture or period of the neighborhood or house. The yard of this Colonial home in the Georgetown section of Washington, D.C., has a fence that matches the house style.

that landscaping should look and feel like an integral part of the surroundings—like it has always been there.

I am of the "natural-look" school, which doesn't mean I don't like a groomed, well-cared-for yard with cultivated plants and formal sitting, living, and entertaining areas. I just want the landscaping to fit like an old shoe. To achieve that, I use indigenous materials: stone that's found in the region (see the top photo at right); man-made pavers and blocks that blend with the colors of the natural surroundings; some native plants; and fencing, lighting, and

paving patterns that are in keeping with the architecture or period of the house or neighborhood (see the bottom photo at right).

I drew a landscape plan for a Vermont client who built a home on a mountainside that resembled a Greek temple. Luckily, it was situated on several hundred acres of land, completely segregated from the rest of the rural, white-clapboard farmhouses of the area. Though I tried as hard as I could to integrate the structure with its site, it still took on a Disneyworldish appearance. You want the land-scaping to feel, look, and be lived

Urban landscapes are usually solitary, with each house having its own little plan.

DEFINING THE YARD

Post-and-rail fencing defines this rural yard, setting off the mowed area from the "wild" areas.

in; you don't want it to look like a Hollywood set. Think of the landscaping as outdoor rooms—extensions of the inside—where you spend leisure and fun time.

The big picture

What surrounds your yard? To get an idea of how your house looks within the neighborhood, step across the street or into a neighbor's yard and look at your house as part of a whole scheme. Start with the fringes of the landscape, the borders or limits of your scope, and then work your way back to the foundation of the house. This exercise will ultimately help you focus on the small parts of your yard and then put them in perspective with the whole scheme.

What you do with your landscape will depend on where you live, whether it's in suburbia, a city, or the country. Large yards may blend from house to house in suburbia, so doing something out of sync with the neighborhood will really stand out. An urban landscape will usually be solitary, each house its own little plan (see the photo above left). Often, that is by necessity as well as by design. A country home with acreage may be so expansive that it requires some enclosure, such as post-and-rail fencing or shrubs or small trees, to create a more intimate yard space or to set the landscaped area off from the wild space (see the drawing at left).

Formal or informal

As I said before, the yard is a reflection of the homeowner. The way you arrange the plants, the shape of the gardens and patio or deck, the types of materials you use, and the pattern in which you set the materials not only work

STRAIGHT WALK, CURVED WALK

Straight walkways and planting beds accentuate the uniform lines of the house and make the yard more formal.

Curved walkways and planting beds mimic nature's way and soften the straight lines of the house.

together to determine the degree of formality or informality of the yard, but they also say something about the owners.

For instance, most curved and serpentine shapes imply a relaxed, informal lifestyle, mimicking nature's way. Flowing lines are found with a meandering brook, with the undulating edge of a forest, and in the graceful sweep of a hillside. A landscape that incorporates those lines will ebb and flow with the surrounding environment and break up the uniform lines and angles of the house (see the drawings above).

A formal look is one in which nature is "controlled." The lines of gardens, walkways, and patios are straight and symmetrical, and shrubs are kept trimmed. This technique is very effective for formal architecture, such as Georgian and Federal style, which beg for symmetrical lines, trimmed

A formal house begs for symmetry and formal gardens.

hedges, and formal gardens (see the photo above).

CONSIDERING CLIMATE

Analyses of the yard and neighborhood are keys to a well-designed landscape, but you also must look at the climate in which you live. The U.S. Department of

Agriculture (USDA) has divided North America into planting regions, called hardiness zones, that indicate a range of the average minimum temperatures in any given area.

Plants are assigned zone designations based on tests conducted by researchers and hybridizers. Nurseries, garden centers, and landscapers attempt to grow, plant, or sell only those plants that will live or perform well in their particular hardiness zone.

To find out which hardiness zone you live in, see the USDA Plant Hardiness Zone Map on p. 160. Choose plants for your yard that are tagged "hardy" for your zone. These plants should stand up well in your landscape year-round. If you choose plants that are borderline hardy for your zone, they will probably need winter protection in cold climates (see the photo below) or sun protection in hot climates. For information about specific plantings, talk to your landscaper or the local garden-center staff.

Microclimates

Within each hardiness zone are microclimates, areas in which climatic conditions differ from surrounding areas. Microclimates can be created by natural conditions or by man.

A lake may moderate the temperature of areas immediately surrounding it. A microclimate such as this may be a whole zone warmer in the wintertime than other areas in the same hardiness zone. Around Lake Champlain, for instance, the autumn is longer, but if the lake freezes, the winter is prolonged as well, although it is usually less severe in temperature than in areas away from the lake.

In the city, the heat of asphalt, masonry, and metal can elevate temperatures considerably. Temperatures even vary from street level to the tops of cars, and above. In fact, one study done in New York City showed the temperature over the roofs of cars to be 10°F to 15°F higher than the surrounding temperature.

WIND TUNNEL

Wind can create a cold microclimate in a small, open area of the yard and could dry out shrubs planted in its path.

In a cold climate, plants that are borderline hardy will require winter protection. Mulch will keep the roots warm, and burlap wrapped around the plant will protect it from the wind and sun.

Your yard probably has more than one microclimate. An unusual wind pattern may make a portion of the yard colder (see the drawing on the facing page), while a very protected space within a fence or courtyard, a corner niche where two walls meet (see the drawing at right), or even the foundation of the house may create warm microclimates.

Big influences on microclimates in your yard are sun and shade patterns. As you look over your site, analyze these patterns. The heaviest shade will be on the north side of trees and houses, but watch the way the shadows travel around, depending on the time of day and the season (see the drawing below). Unless the house is on a perfect compass point, the shadiest orientation may allow a few hours of morning or afternoon sun, the latter being of greater intensity. This might be a great spot for a patio or a deck, which will enjoy both sun and shade.

What may appear to be the best place for a plant because it is sunny and open may, in fact, be the harshest place. Not only will the temperature in this spot be higher than the surrounding temperature during summer, but the plant will also receive harsh winter sun and wind.

Unfortunately, there are no guidebooks or hardiness zone maps for your yard. It is possible to encounter a microclimate anywhere. If a hardy plant is not performing well, it may be that it is sitting in an unsuitable microclimate. The solution is to move the plant to a different spot to see if it thrives there.

WARM NICHE

Where the two walls of this home meet is a warm microclimate. This area would be a good place to experiment with planting borderline-hardy plants.

SHADE PATTERNS

Unless your house is on a perfect compass point, shade patterns will travel around trees, depending on the time of day. The shade patterns may affect what plants you can grow successfully and where you locate patios, pools, or decks.

9 A.M.

Noon

3 P.M.

CHAPTER 4

The Landscape Plan

E ven the simplest project requires some planning, and, indeed, benefits by design and engineering. When driving a car, you follow a route. When cooking a meal, you follow a recipe or at least devise the dish in your head. Likewise, when landscaping the yard, you should follow a plan.

Design informs even the simplest structure, whether of brick-and-steel or of prose. You raise a pup tent from one vision, a cathedral from another. This does not mean that you must sit with a blueprint always in front of you, merely that you had best anticipate what you are getting into.

(E. B. White, *Elements of Style*)

When planning a landscape, don't be afraid to scour what's already out there for inspiration. I must confess that some of my best designs were inspired by photos of landscapes in magazines and books, by features I've seen in other landscapes, or by just observing nature's shapes. I once designed a fence based on a photo I took of an old barn with a stone foundation and board-and-batten siding above that. From that inspiration, I built a rustic fence with a 2-ft.-high dry-laid stone wall topped with 4 ft. of gray-stained, board-and-batten cedar fencing with the posts actually embedded in the wall. Lesson learned: If the idea looks good to you somewhere else, it's probably because it is a design that works and is worth adapting to fit your needs.

The picture of what you want your landscape to look like and how you want it to function was started when you began the evaluation of your yard. Up to this point, you have determined existing grade and have corrected it, if necessary.

You've tested the soil and have made certain it can nourish plants appropriate to your hardiness zone. You have talked with family members about their needs and know how the yard will be used. And you are clear on how to integrate the character and style of the neighborhood and your home into the new landscape. Now you are ready to create a working landscape plan.

TAKING MEASUREMENTS

If you haven't already done so, draw freehand a bird's-eye view of the house, yard, and any existing landscape features you plan on keeping (there is absolutely no need for accuracy at this point), then go outside and measure them.

For most of the measurements, you can use a long tape measure (to make the job easier, ask a friend or family member to help you). But for the longer perimeter yard measurements, a walk-beside measuring wheel will work better (you can borrow one at a rental center).

Begin by measuring the house (see the drawing below). Start at the corners and measure in. Mark

HOUSE MEASUREMENTS

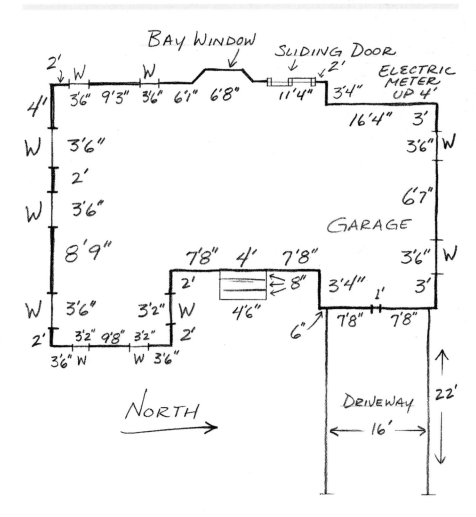

locations of all windows and doors, steps, decks, and patios in the drawing. Measure and label the garage and driveway as well. These measurements don't have to be exact—they just have to be close.

Be careful with angled surfaces that are created by bay windows and other irregularly shaped house protrusions; they are tricky to measure. But I found a simple way to estimate that is pretty close (see the drawing below), and that's all you need.

First butt a straightedge against the wall, perpendicular to the house, at the end of the window. Then stretch the tape measure to the straightedge from the corner where the middle glass pane meets the side pane. Measure the distance from the

intersection point to the window corner and to the house, and measure the middle pane. Then plot these distances on the drawing. These measurements will give you a good idea of the length of the window and how far it projects out into the yard.

Once you have all the house measurements on paper, measure to the outlying structures or landscape features you are keeping, using the house as your anchor for measuring (see the drawing on the facing page).

Start from the corners of the house. For instance, to measure to a couple of outlying trees, start at a corner, walk straight ahead in one direction until you are aligned with the middle of the closest tree, and

then record that measurement. Then measure straight from that point to the center of the tree and write down the measurement. Walk straight out in one direction until you are aligned with the center of the second tree and record that measurement. Then measure and record the distance from that point to the center of the second tree. Repeat this procedure for all outlying objects.

ORGANIZING THE DESIGN

Once you have the measurements of the existing design on the rough drawing, you can use it to help organize the new design to make all the components work together. How you arrange the landscape elements in your yard is really a matter of personal taste. But when organizing your ideas, you should consider composition, scale, balance, color, and texture. It's best to work on this part of the plan while you're still outside.

Composition

Your first goal in designing the plan should be achieving good composition. How will the separate components relate to each other— the walkway to the front door, the planting beds to the walkway, a retaining wall to the planting beds—and how will they work together to create a pleasing landscape?

The difference between a design that looks professional and one that looks amateurish is in how the separate components work together. For instance, in a front yard, a planting bed should not be treated as a separate entity, nor should the walkway, or even a tree. Integrating the outside lines of the

MEASURING ANGLED SURFACES

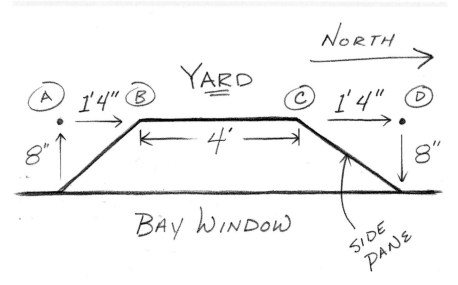

1. Measure out from the house to points A and D to find out how far the window projects into the yard.

2. Measure from A to B, from D to C, and from C to B to find the width of the window.

MEASURING TO OUTLYING OBJECTS

1. Record the measurement from the house corner straight out to point A, which is aligned with the center of the first tree.

2. Measure from point A to the center of the first tree, point B.

3. Measure straight out from point B to the point that aligns with the center of the second tree, point C.

4. Measure straight out from point C to the center of the second tree, point D.

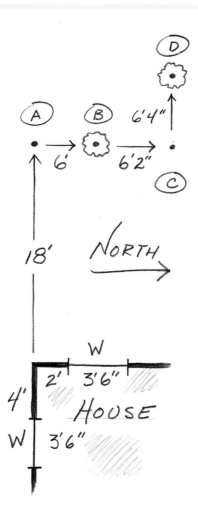

planting bed with the parameters of the walkway makes one smooth line and links the two components. The tree should balance with plantings near it or be incorporated into a bed to tie it to the planting bed near the walkway.

At this point it's also important to analyze the big picture if you haven't already done so. Consider how the composition of the yard will relate to the house and how the house and yard will relate to the entire neighborhood. It may be necessary to step into the street or into a neighbor's yard to take in the entire composition. You may want to use props such as a flexible garden hose or stakes and string to lay out lines on the ground for walkways, planting beds, or patios (see the photo below).

As you're walking around the yard, write down ideas or sketch them out so that you remember them when you are ready to begin drawing the landscape plan.

To help visualize the lines of curved walkways, patios, or planting beds, use a prop. Here, a garden hose helps to outline a planting bed.

Splay the walkway where it meets the driveway or street to make it inviting and to soften the harsh meeting of perpendicular lines.

Scale and balance

Next, consider how the new landscape components will relate in scale and balance to the existing components of the yard.

For example, if you are adding a walkway, think about its size and shape in relation to the size and shape of the house and yard. Is the walkway the right size for the entry? Is it too small, too narrow, too unimportant in relation to the house and yard? Or is it too big, claiming too much attention? Will it be curved or straight? And how will the walkway meet the street or the driveway where it originates?

Splaying or flaring a walkway at its origination or destination makes it inviting and softens the harsh meeting of perpendicular lines (see the photo above).

Consider the shapes of all the components and think about how they relate to one another. Do you want an informal yard, with lots of curves throughout, or do you want a formal yard with straight lines? Maybe you want a combination of both. If you prefer a straight walkway but don't want a totally formal yard, add curved planting beds and arrange plants in a serpentine manner to

relax the straight lines of the house and the walkway.

Is symmetry the look you want, or do you prefer an asymmetrical look? For instance, if you are putting plantings on both sides of a walkway, do you want them to be the same size and shape? Or would you prefer to place a tall, pointy plant on one side and balance it on the other side with three short, round plants? I think the latter design provides more interest because of the contrast.

It's also important to look at the house facade and foundation. Look

Cool blues recede in the landscape while hot colors draw attention.

for areas where you can place planting beds close to the house to conceal the foundation. Also look for places near the house where planting beds can be pulled away to add depth and perspective. If you want tall plantings to add interest to the horizontal walls, look for breaks in the house facade and locate the taller plants where they won't block window views.

Color

After thinking about composition, scale, and balance, next consider what colors you want to incorporate into your design and how to make them work together. Colored plantings spice up a yard and add depth to your design. But with myriad colors from which to choose, figuring out what you want can seem overwhelming.

I can't give you any hard-and-fast rules, but remember that cool colors—blues, greens, and pastels—recede in the landscape, while warm colors—reds, oranges, and yellows—stand out. When you place warm colors to the rear of a planting bed, you will add dimension or depth to the image because your eyes will be drawn toward the back of the bed gradually as they catch the color. Similarly, if you repeat the warm color, say red, every few feet, your eyes will be drawn across the planting bed, allowing you to take in the whole picture.

Combine whites and reds with dark greens. Shades of purple work well with pinks and bright yellows (see the photo above). But don't feel like you must be conservative when combining colors. Experiment. Take risks. Time and again clients insist that I not use orange or a combination of orange and purple. But in the right spot, this is a gorgeous combination—my bright orange poppies look spectacular next to my purple-edged white iris.

And in spring, after a dark, dreary, cold winter, there is no better combination to brighten and warm the feel of the yard.

Texture

When designing a landscape, use textures to draw the eye and to create a mood. If textures are combined correctly, you should be able to "feel" them with your eyes.

Texture can be a difficult concept to grasp. If your are having trouble, try this: Close your eyes and try to feel with your mind. Imagine touching smooth moss and then a rough brick walkway, or envision looking at a smooth weeping willow next to a needled spruce tree.

Simple texture differences—like tall, spiky flowers combined with round, daisylike flowers, evergreens with deciduous trees, smooth slate combined with rough concrete, bark mulch and gravel—contribute to a diversity of sensations that delight the eyes and enhance the composition, scale, balance, and colors you have chosen for your design.

DRAWING UP THE PLAN

With a clear picture of how your landscape will be organized, you're now ready to sit down inside and draw up the working plan. The first step is to draw to scale the existing landscape. From that drawing, you can create the new design.

DRAWING TOOLS

Before beginning, you'll need to purchase a few drawing tools. Graph paper makes it pretty easy to make scale drawings—tracing paper or vellum makes the job a little more adventurous.

My mother always said to use a pencil for crossword puzzles—nobody is that good the first time. And the same rule applies here, but keep the pencil sharp and have a good eraser on hand. I change my mind often and make mistakes here and there, so I have an electric eraser that gets more use than my toothbrush.

A ruler will help you measure and draw straight lines. If you have not chosen graph paper, you'll need an architect's or engineer's scale, which makes it easy to create scale drawings and can also serve as a straightedge.

To make perfect circles, you may want to have on hand a few circle templates of varying size, from small to large, a template with plant shapes, or a compass (drawing circles freehand should work just fine, though). To create serpentine lines of any shape, I use a flexible curve, a tool made of rubber-coated lead.

Drawing tools make it easier to put the plans on paper. From top to bottom: a pencil sharpener, draftsman's triangle, scales, lead pencil, templates, compass, masking tape, and a flexible curve.

To draw straight lines, align two straightedges perpendicular to one another, using the edge of the table as a guide.

Start with the old

The first thing to do is to make a scale drawing of the existing yard, including only elements you plan on keeping. To keep the paper from sliding around as you draw, attach the corners to the table with masking tape. To ensure that the paper is straight, measure up evenly from the edge of the table when affixing the paper, making sure it's parallel to the table edge.

With that done, transfer the house and yard measurements—keeping them in scale—from the rough drawing to the paper. If you're using graph paper, this is easy. Simply assign a dimension to each box: For example, if 2 ft. is equal to one box, a 10-ft. section of the house or yard could be drawn to scale simply by connecting five boxes on the graph paper.

With an architect's scale, measurements are assigned to 1-in. increments. For instance, a 1:8 scale means 1 in. equals 8 ft. An engineer's scale works the same way, but it uses larger increments, such as 1 in. equals 10 ft. or 1 in. equals 20 ft. With a 1:20 scale, a whole acre could fit on one 8-in. by 11-in. sheet of paper. I typically use a 1:8 architect's scale or 1:10 engineer's scale for residential plans. To get a close view of one section of the yard, I use a 1:4 architect's scale.

From the rough drawing, add up the horizontal measurements and then the vertical measurements to get totals. This will help locate the house so that it fits on the paper in the right place. If there is more front yard than back, the house should be drawn toward the back of the paper, and vice versa.

To ensure that all the lines you draw on the paper are straight, lay a straightedge vertically against the edge of the table and place another one horizontally, perpendicular to the vertical one (see the photo above). Create right angles at the house corners using the same method.

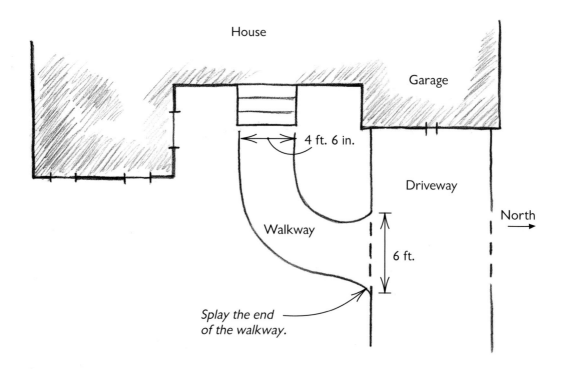

If all of this is too detailed for you, and if you don't mind if the house looks like a trapezoid, then don't worry about it. An out-of-square, slightly off-scale drawing will only be a problem if it will be used to figure out engineering specs, material needs, or cost estimates. Simple planting plans don't require the same level of accuracy.

Add the new

After putting all the existing elements on paper, make a U-turn. Totally clear your mind of any preconceived ideas and forget what your yard looks like now. If the fundamental parts of the front yard landscape exist, like a walkway and planting beds, try to ignore them. Pretend you're working with a blank slate. Be limited only by how far your imagination can go. Take risks and explore options you have never dreamed possible.

Place a piece of tracing paper over the existing layout and play with the spaces. Find the beginning and end of the walkway: Curve it, loop it—draw a veritable yellow brick road. Make a walkway that is in scale with the house, and be generous with its width—allow at least 4 ft. for two people to walk comfortably side by side (see the drawing above). Pull the walkway out from the house, leaving plenty of space for planting beds in between. When you're satisfied with the design, transfer your sketch to the scale drawing.

Experiment with shapes for decks and patios as well as for planting beds and vegetable gardens. Oval, kidney, or free-form shapes make it easier to combine elements than squares and rectangles. As you finish designing each component, transfer the sketch to the scale drawing.

When drawing a deck or patio, remember to leave room for furniture—the barbecue, the dining table and chairs, chaise lounges—and for people. It helps to make scale cutouts of all the furniture so you can move them around on your drawing to get an accurate picture of the space (see the photo on p. 34).

Take advantage of existing shade trees. Look at the shade patterns you studied earlier and place the patio in a comfortable spot in the shade. Also, place the pool and play areas away from shaded spaces.

When planning the planting beds and vegetable gardens, remember the dog's habits and try to place these spots out of the way of the dog. Draw the beds with serpentine edges that meander along the walk-way and tie back into the walls of the house, wrapping around the

ADDING A PLANTING BED

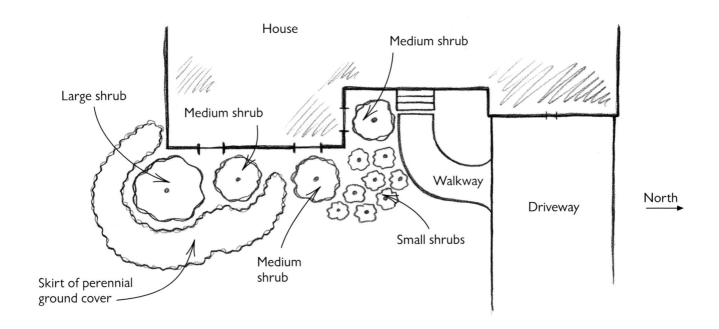

House

Medium shrub

Large shrub

Medium shrub

Medium shrub

Walkway

North

Driveway

Small shrubs

Skirt of perennial
ground cover

corners (see the drawing above). Draw them wide enough to have layers of plantings—short ones in front of tall ones—skirts of ground covers, and big flares for small trees you wouldn't want too close to the house. Use the windows of the house to help locate the beds, and think about what you want to see from inside the house. Go wild with the planting beds. Don't limit yourself. The planting beds can always be scaled back to fit the budget and then augmented later according to this plan.

Choosing plants

Once you have the main components of the landscape drawn in scale on the plan, it's time to get down to details: choosing and arranging plants, including trees, shrubs, and flowers.

Get out your plant books and make a list of your favorite plants. Of course, only list those appropriate

for the exposure—whether it be sun or shade—and the hardiness zone you live in. Decide how much upkeep you are interested in doing, and consider drought tolerance, pruning requirements, and disease and pest resistance. Pay attention to ultimate heights and spreads when choosing plants that are next to the house or plants that will be located under electric lines or near the perimeters of the yard.

Again, use a piece of tracing paper over the layout, and draw circles to represent the plants. Draw them to their mature sizes, so you can see how close to place them.

Plants look more natural when used in odd numbers. One specimen or three plants in a group works better than two or four because it looks less contrived, more natural. If there is a good spot for a focal point at the turn of a walkway

or at the end of an allée, choose a plant with an eye-catching shape or color.

Add layers of perennials, annuals, or ground covers in front of shrubs and around the bottom of trees (see the drawing on p. 44), and dress up bare walls with vines. Pick plants for year-round interest and color—winter berries or sculptural branching, spring or summer flowers, and fall foliage colors. If one plant is at its best in spring, make sure the one next to it has another season of interest so that something will be happening throughout the year. Use repetition of color, shape, or actual plants to draw the eye from one side of the planting bed to the other. Repetition—which is what the professionals do—integrates the whole picture and makes the composition successful.

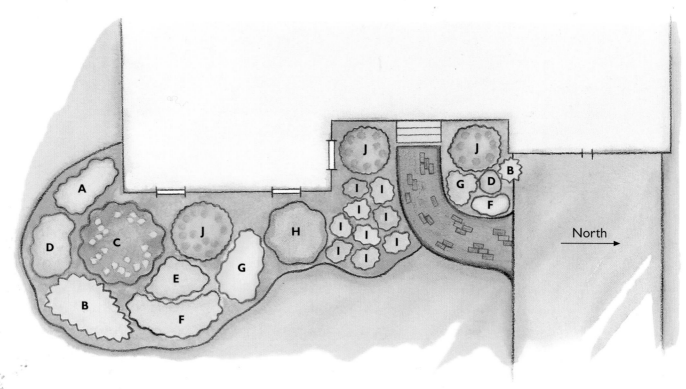

A	*Rudbeckia* 'Goldsturm'	**F**	*Chrysanthemum* 'Snowcap'
B	Daylily 'Stella D'Oro'	**G**	*Coreopsis* 'Moonbeam'
C	*Viburnum* 'Mariesii'	**H**	Seagreen juniper
D	*Liatris* 'Kobold'	**I**	*Euonymus* 'Emerald Gaiety'
E	*Salvia* 'East Friesland'	**J**	*Weigela* 'Rhumba'

Make sure all of your plant choices are available at the local garden center or through a catalog. You should also be aware of growth rates so that individual plants within the landscape will mature at the rate you want them to. If you buy young, slow-growing plants, such as dwarf conifers, and combine them with older, fast-growing plants, such as deciduous flowering shrubs, the more vigorous plants will outgrow the slower ones in no time. Here's where budget comes into play. Although a slower-growing plant is usually more expensive, you should buy an older, larger one and cut back on the sizes or quantities of fast-growing plants. This will not only balance the budget, but it will also help keep your landscape in balance.

Also, keep in mind that unlike an interior-designed room in your home, which looks its best the day the furniture arrives, the landscaping in the yard will be at its peak 5 to 10 years from the day of installation. You can minimize or maximize that time period depending on your budget. If you have more money to spend and can start with larger plants, they will mature in less time, and the landscape will be at its peak in a shorter amount of time.

If you find that all of this detail work is overwhelming, that the rough sketch is about all you can handle, or that you are having trouble putting all your great ideas to paper, you may want to hire a landscape designer or architect who will skillfully translate your ideas to pictures. For help in finding the right professional, see Chapter 12.

CHAPTER 5

A Retaining-Wall Primer

I once gave a design talk to a group of rhododendron growers in Columbus, Ohio. When I came to my slides about retaining walls and began to speak on the basics of building them correctly, a hand shot up in the audience. "Haven't you noticed, Jane, there is no slope in Columbus. We don't need retaining walls."

Rip-rap can be used to form an excellent and inexpensive retaining system. Planting pockets are left between the rocks to add interest.

GENERAL GUIDELINES

When planning a retaining wall, the four things you need to address up front are its height, length, shape, and width.

Ideally, a retaining wall should not exceed 4 ft. in height. If you have a slope that is higher than 4 ft., you'd be better off constructing a terraced system of retaining walls if you have the space. That's because retaining walls that are higher than 4 ft. typically require advanced building techniques and utilize high-tech materials to help the wall withstand the pressure of a lot of earth and water. High retaining walls really only belong along highways or in small-space gardens where there is no distance to terrace the land.

The only limitation for the wall's length is to satisfy the retainage of the slope and to best exploit the materials being used. It is not advisable to stop a retaining wall short of completing the job or without solidly propping and securing the timbers, stone, or other material being used.

Both shape and width depend on what is providing the main infrastructure of the wall. For instance, landscape timbers make a straight or geometrically angled wall, and while they may be the narrowest of materials, the underground reinforcement structure that provides their integrity is actually wider than a dry-laid stone retaining wall. Rip-rap, concrete wall systems, and dry-laid stone walls can be curved or straight, and width will vary with height and materials.

After reddening with embarrassment from my seeming unpreparedness and lack of observation, I recovered by reminding the audience that although retaining walls are used mostly to ease or hide a severe slope, they can also be used for decorative purposes.

People like to incorporate retaining walls into their yards for many reasons. As I mentioned in Chapter 1, some people may need to hide or lessen the severity of a sloped yard. Other folks may have homes with too much foundation showing, causing the house to pop out of the ground visually, so they incorporate in the landscape a retaining wall with a raised planting bed that shields the foundation. Many gardeners like to plant in raised beds because they are attractive and ease the strain of working at ground level. Some homeowners just want an excuse to build a stone wall because they like them.

There are four types of retaining-wall systems that I prefer: rip-rap walls, timber walls, concrete wall systems, and dry-laid stone walls. Regardless of the type you choose, there are a few building guidelines that apply to all of them.

RIP-RAP WALLS

Boulders can be used to form an excellent and inexpensive retaining system that I call rip-rap (see the drawing at right). Because of the size and weight of the boulders, building this type of wall may require renting a skid-steer loader to put the boulders in place (you'll also need pry bars and a shovel). But rip-rap is a very natural, long-lived, and attractive way to retain the earth. The boulders are dug into the slope, and planting pockets can be left between them to add color and texture and to make the wall blend in with the natural landscape (see the photo on the facing page).

Rip-rap is a perfect solution for a rather severe slope that graduates back as it rises, has been a maintenance nightmare, or has caused an erosion problem. Terracing with rip-rap can be difficult, unless there is ample room on the flat plateaus between the levels to anchor machinery and to build the next level. The terraces will have to be carefully graded ahead of time to allow for the flat plateaus between.

Steps may be incorporated into the design, but the areas where they will be located must be graded to accommodate them. Save long, flat boulders for steps. Keep the stair height (rise) comfortable (6 in. to 8 in.) and dig in any boulders that are thicker than that. I like to meander steps through rip-rap, which is a little more difficult to execute, but it's a very natural way to move up and down the slope.

RIP-RAP

Boulders form an inexpensive retaining-wall system called rip-rap. Steps can be incorporated into a rip-rap wall, and plants are placed around the boulders. When the slope is gradual, boulders can be placed farther apart. On a severe slope, boulders should be spaced closer together.

Finding boulders

You can get boulders from local farmers who rid their fields of them and often have stockpiles on their property. You will probably have to provide a truck, but you may be able to persuade the farmer to load it with his tractor, for a price or a barter, of course.

Another place to get boulders is from a quarry, which cuts different types and sizes of stone. The type you can get depends on where the quarry is located. You will pay by the ton or sometimes by the cubic yard for the material, and you'll also pay for the trucking.

To determine how many cubic yards of boulders you will need, measure the square footage of the slope, divide by 27 (the number of feet in a cubic yard), and subtract about 10% for planting space between the boulders. Order by the cubic yard, and someone at the quarry will figure the conversion to tons for the density of material you choose.

Ideally, rip-rap should be made from rounded boulders at least the size of a charcoal kettle grill. Squarer boulders will work, but the final look may be more of a rock outcropping (see the photo below). Whenever possible, use boulders that are indigenous to your area (or at least look like they are). Rip-rap should disappear in the landscape, not become the focal point by looking out of place. The plants placed between the boulders should be the accent that draws the eye, not the boulders themselves.

Placing the boulders

After grading the slope correctly, prepare it by removing any leftover sod and weeds, either with hand tools or, in larger areas, with a nonresidual, systemic herbicide like Round-up. On a high, steep slope, the boulders should be placed close together. If the slope is gradual and fairly low, the boulders should be placed farther apart.

As I said before, rip-rap walls may require a skid-steer loader equipped with a bucket and forks (like those of a forklift). You can rent one on a daily or weekly basis. Building rip-rap walls is hard work and requires at least two people to help move the boulders, so ask friends or family members to help.

A typical skid-steer loader will only handle 1,200 lb. or less. If your boulders are very large, it may be necessary to hire a landscaper, who can install the boulders with a larger machine like a backhoe or bucket loader. If the slope makes safe access difficult, you may want to hire a contractor to install the boulders. To save costs, you can offer to be the helper.

A severe slope can be retained with square boulders placed to look like natural outcroppings.

Here's how to build a rip-rap wall. Use the bucket of the skid-steer loader to dig out the spots for the boulders (this job could also be done by hand or with the forks of the machine). You can expect to dig in or bury each boulder up to one-third its thickness. Then put the forks on the machine to carry the boulders to their locations. With the help of a pry bar, direct the boulders into place (see the drawing at right)—some tweaking with the pry bar may be required to get the boulder to sit correctly.

Start building from the bottom up. Stack the boulders in a somewhat random way, although the best rip-rap is fitted and matched without appearing obviously "done." Part of the job is picking which side of the boulder looks best and making that the exposed face. Another aspect is trying to get the boulder to fit with the ones next to it or above it. As the stack builds, all faces should look similar and be directed in a similar direction so that no one stands out. This increases the subtlety of the structure and looks more natural. If there is a particularly interesting face you like, and it doesn't fit with the other boulders, try to place it where it can become a focal point or accent, much like a brightly colored plant would stand out among dark-colored plants. I have found boulders with veins of quartz or with interesting nooks and crannies and placed them where I knew they would be seen and appreciated.

I mentioned digging in the boulders: it is essential not only for stabilizing the boulders in the ground but also for decreasing

RIP-RAP IN PROGRESS

Use the forks of the skid-steer loader to transport the large boulders. As you near the boulder's intended spot in the wall, lower the forks and have a partner use a pry bar to move the boulder into place.

potential erosion problems when water runs down the slope and for making them look like a part of the earth, not teetering on top. You'll also find that digging in the boulders will help you prop them in the direction you want and will help expose the faces at the proper angle. Try to direct the faces a little upwards because people will be looking down or directly at the finished product.

TIMBER WALLS

I choose landscape timbers as retaining material when I want a straight or angled wall, when there is no room to terrace, or when there is a limited budget.

Buying materials

I prefer using pressure-treated timbers, either 6x6s or 8x8s. I do not recommend railroad ties for any use. They are not uniform in shape or size, as they are usually well worn from use, and the creosote with which they are treated burns skin and ruins clothing. I don't like the crude look and dark color, either. It really stands out.

To retain a long, gradual slope, you may elect to step the height of the timber wall at regular intervals or with the lay of the land, which may reduce the amount of materials and backfill needed. More involved walls can incorporate steps and planting boxes in their structure, which will add to the amount of materials needed.

To plan and purchase the materials, figure the length and height of the wall for the amount of timbers running parallel to the slope. Add to that the number of timbers needed for reinforcement (timber walls are reinforced on every other level with 4-ft. timbers called deadmen). You will need a heavy-duty 16-in. circular saw to cut the timbers (which can be rented). I don't even consider using a chainsaw because the cuts are crude, making a smooth, gapless meeting of the timbers impossible. You'll also need a drill large enough to accommodate a ⅝-in. spade bit, which is used to start holes for the 12-in. common spikes that tie the timbers together; a level; 12d common galvanized nails and a hammer to toenail timbers together; ¾-in. washed gravel for drainage; and plastic filter fabric.

It is always a good idea to protect yourself from the sawdust of pressure-treated wood by using a dust mask and gloves. Shield your eyes from flying debris with safety glasses and use ear protection when operating any loud machinery, like a power saw.

Building the wall

Constructing a timber retaining wall is not a lazy person's job (see the drawing below). You first must dig a trench that is 12 in. deep by 12 in. to 18 in. wide and fill it with 6 in. to 12 in. of ¾-in. gravel. This will serve as a wide base for the wall. Make sure that the gravel is compacted well with a hand tamper or a plate compactor before you place the first timbers. You may need to adjust the base to level the first timbers.

The key ingredient of a timber retaining wall is the infrastructure, or cribbing, behind it that provides the integrity of the structure and prevents it from buckling. Tie every other level of the wall back into the slope with reinforcing timbers

TIMBER RETAINING WALL

Use 6x6 or 8x8 pressure-treated timbers and step the wall to follow the slope.

Timber anchors the deadmen.

Filter fabric is placed behind the wall (not shown).

Base of ¾-in. washed gravel

6 in.

18 in.

Deadmen reinforce the structure.

Bevel the ends of the exposed timbers for a smooth finish.

12-in. common spikes spaced about every 2 ft. secure the timbers.

Toenail deadmen in place.

Bevel the exposed ends of a timber retaining wall for a neater finish and no protruding corners.

called deadmen, which run perpendicular to the wall. When you see a deteriorating wall, look for deadmen, and I bet you'll not see a one. Many a timber retaining wall has lurched forward from the weight of earth and water because it lacked that structure behind it.

The length of the deadmen is determined by the height of the wall: The taller the wall, the longer the deadmen. For instance, a 4-ft.-high wall should be anchored at 4-ft. intervals with deadmen that are 6 ft. to 8 ft. long. A 2-ft.-high wall would require deadmen that are 4 ft. to 6 ft. long and spaced farther apart. Spike the deadmen to the wall and then fasten them together at their ends with a timber running parallel to the wall.

Place the filter fabric against the back of the timbers, with a 6-in.- to 12-in.-wide layer of ¾-in. gravel added behind the fabric. The gravel facilitates drainage, and the fabric lets water through but keeps silt from infiltrating the timbers. After adding the gravel and fabric, backfill with soil.

Backfill after placing each level of timbers to make it easier to level the deadmen and the supporting timber. Place the deadmen, beginning with the second level.

Attach the levels by drilling holes and driving the spikes down through the timbers at each level. To hold the timbers in place for drilling and spiking, toenail them at the ends. Although most of the toenails will not show once the

structure is finished, remove any nails that would be exposed. For strength, alternate the joints and deadmen so that no joints are directly on top of one another. As a finish detail, bevel-cut the exposed ends of the timber using the circular saw (see the photo above). This will provide a smooth transition to the earth and will also prevent people from bumping into a sharp corner.

If you are unfamiliar with saws and carpentry, it is advisable to hire a contractor or a professional landscaper for this work. You may be able to provide the brawn the contractor needs and learn a lot at the same time. If the structure will integrate steps and planting boxes, a detailed plan should be drawn by a professional to minimize waste and to maximize the potential of the space and timbers. The plan should include a materials list, so you can buy efficiently and economically.

CONCRETE WALL SYSTEMS

Less expensive and labor intensive than building a stone wall, concrete wall systems offer homeowners a more tailored, easy-to-construct alternative to stone walls (see the photo below). Concrete wall systems can be designed with curves, both outside and inverse radii, and can be ordered in many shapes and colors. For this job you'll need some simple tools: a shovel (or skid-steer loader), a plate compac-

tor, a few rakes, and a partner saw, which is a circular saw with a stone-cutting or diamond blade.

I have yet to find a manufacturer with a system reliable enough to go higher than 4 ft., although many make claims otherwise. The more industrial systems used on highway embankments incorporate oversized blocks and detailed infrastructures, out of scale with the usual home-owner project. Some systems look like split granite blocks with rough faces, while others are smooth and have curved faces. The main body blocks are usually about 8 in. thick with ridges on the top and grooves on the bottom to fit the stones together (see the top right photo on the facing page). Some use fiberglass pins to hold the blocks

together (see the top left photo on the facing page). Most systems provide capstones to provide a smooth top surface.

Follow the manufacturer's recommendations for materials and the amount needed for your project. You will need to know the finished length and height of the wall to make the calculations.

The most important part of the job is preparing the base (see the bottom photo on the facing page). You will need to dig a trench to make a level base for the wall, at least 1 ft. deep and 2 ft. to 3 ft. wide, depending on the size of the blocks. A small backhoe or shovel with muscle behind it will do the job. Fill the trench with ¾-in.

A concrete wall system looks less artificial when the capping is done with natural bluestone. The step risers here are made of the same block as the walls, and the treads are made of bluestone.

Concrete wall systems fit together differently, depending on the manufacturer. The system above has interlocking ridges and grooves. The infrastructure of the system at left is held together with fiberglass pins and netting.

gravel (not peastone, which is only one size aggregate), which will pack well with a plate compactor. Compact halfway through the backfilling, then again when the trench is full, and check for level constantly and adjust, if needed. Once you have placed the first row of blocks and have checked them for level, the rest is easy.

As the wall builds in height, place plastic filter fabric behind it, adding 6 in. to 12 in. of ¾-in. washed gravel behind that (see the drawing on p. 54). The blocks are porous and will allow the soil to drain. Any of the systems need continuous backfill for structural integrity, so backfill after each level goes up.

Cap the wall with the manufacturer's capstones or with a flat, natural stone like bluestone or slate (see the photo on the facing page). I use bluestone that's at least 1½ in.

No matter which system you use, it's important to prepare a proper base and make sure the first level of blocks is level.

CONCRETE WALL SYSTEM

With a concrete wall system, a level base and careful backfilling are required, as with other retaining-wall systems, but no guesswork is involved in building the wall itself. Just stack the blocks after the base has been installed. The system has its own locking mechanism to hold the blocks together.

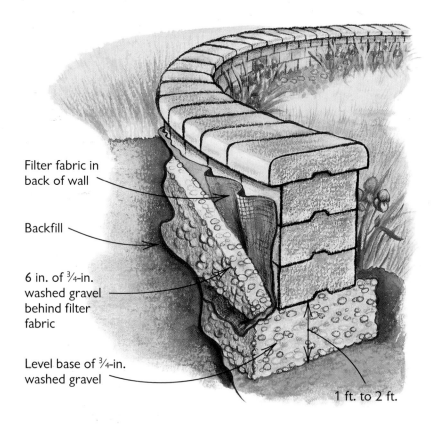

Filter fabric in back of wall

Backfill

6 in. of ¾-in. washed gravel behind filter fabric

Level base of ¾-in. washed gravel

1 ft. to 2 ft.

thick, and I leave it overhanging the top block by about 1 in. To hold the bluestone in place, mastique it to the top level of blocks. Use a partner saw to cut the stone. If the wall is radiused, cut the stone to follow the curve.

Stack the blocks to the desired height, leaving room for the capstones and stepping the blocks on the ends of the wall to follow the slope. One big advantage to concrete wall systems is that some designs allow you to create steps with the blocks through the wall system (see the photo below).

The main difficulties in using concrete wall systems are the weight of the pallets of blocks, which you may need to unload by hand or use a machine to move around, and incorporating the blocks into trickier designs with steps or terracing. With good planning, concrete wall systems should be uncomplicated enough to build without the expertise of a professional.

Steps can be made of the wall material if the blocks are the proper height for step risers. If not, as in this case, granite curbing and pavers are fit between retaining walls.

DRY-LAID STONE WALLS

No scene is more idyllic or evocative of the country than that of a meandering stone wall. Many people love the look but don't appreciate the time and skill involved in building one correctly and for longevity. The stone is not the major cost in this endeavor. It is labor, labor, and more labor, requiring time, concentration, and dedication. Not everyone has the jigsaw puzzle head for this task, either.

You don't need a lot of tools for the job, but some of them are not common (see the photo at right): a brick hammer used for cutting and shaping stone; a large sledgehammer and a smaller one for moving or cutting large stones; pry bars for moving stones; wide chisels for splitting; a level and yardstick; and a tape measure. It's possible to rent these hand tools, but you may be able to borrow from friends. You will also need a way to move the stones around. A hand truck or tree cart and pry bar works; a skid-steer loader is also an option.

I do not like the look of round boulder walls or flat, thin slate walls, but they are perfectly acceptable if you like the look. My preference is fieldstone that's at least 4 in. thick. Stone may be obtained from a local farmer or a quarry, and for this job, square-edged stones cut by a quarry might be better than uncut ones, especially for corners, end stones, and capstones.

Tools needed to build dry-laid stone walls are, from left to right: sledge-hammer, brick hammer, yardstick, small sledgehammer, pry bars, and a large sledgehammer. You'll also need chisels and a level.

Laying out the stones

Spread the stones out on the ground so you can see what you have. Leaving the stones on the ground for a prolonged period will kill the grass and litter the area with stone shards. So choose a place where you don't mind a mess and where eventual re-grading for a lawn or drive-way will not be a problem.

Look for large, flat stones and set them aside for capstones and end stones. Use the largest, most substantial stones for the base. Save stones already cut with 90° angles for the ends and corners of the wall. As you build up the wall, you'll have to search for stones that will fit certain spots. Patience will be very important here.

To split a stone, place it on its side and drive a chisel into one end, just enough to make a crack (above). Then drive another chisel into the opposite end. Then rap the chisels evenly until the stone splits (right).

DRY-LAID STONE WALL

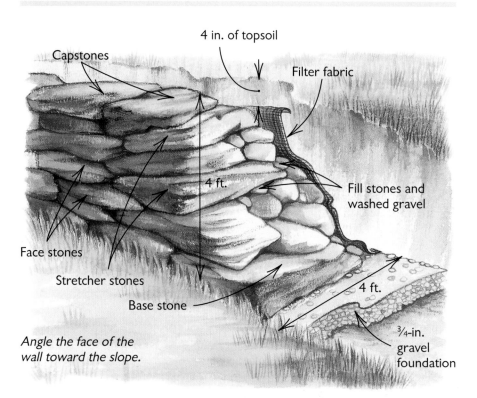

Capstones

4 in. of topsoil

Filter fabric

4 ft.

Fill stones and washed gravel

Face stones

Stretcher stones

Base stone

4 ft.

¾-in. gravel foundation

Angle the face of the wall toward the slope.

The width of the gravel foundation equals the height of the wall. The foundation should be leveled and compacted from front to back.

If you don't have many flatter stones, you can split the ones you have with a hammer and a couple of wide chisels. Look for "splittable" stones—those that are layered evenly. You can see the levels by looking at the grain and color differences on the side of the stone.

When you have a splittable stone, place it on its side and drive a chisel into one end, just enough to make a crack. Then drive another chisel into the opposite end. Then rap the chisels evenly until the stone splits (see the photos above). If you don't hit the chisels evenly, the stone might not split evenly.

Making the footing

As in most retaining-wall systems, dry-laid stone walls require sure footing. The footing of a dry-laid stone wall consists of a gravel foundation and the base stones (see the drawing at left). The footing should be equal in width to the height of the wall. For example, a 4-ft.-high wall should have a

4-ft.-wide footing. The width of this size wall will taper toward the top to about 2 ft. Dig a 1-ft.-deep trench wide enough to accommodate the width of the base and fill it with ¾-in. washed gravel for drainage. Make sure the gravel foundation is level and well compacted.

Building the wall

With the gravel foundation completed, place the large stones you've chosen for the base on top of it. Then start building the wall up from there.

To help keep the wall straight and at the right finished height, string a level line on stakes from one end of the wall to the other (see the top drawing at right). If the wall is curved, use the line and stakes to keep track of the finished level and a flexible garden hose on the ground to outline the curves to be followed.

You must fit stones together perfectly, like a jigsaw puzzle. You'll have to cut some stones using hammers and chisels or a brick hammer (see the bottom drawing at right), but make sure you can't see any raw, chiseled edges on the face of the wall. Intermingle stretcher stones that span the entire distance across the wall with those that don't and cover joints with a full stone on top. Stretcher stones tie the wall to the ground and give integrity to the finished product. Use stones of different thicknesses to give the wall character.

Fill the back of the wall as you go with smaller stones—usually what's unusable for the face of the wall—

BUILDING A LEVEL WALL

String a level line between stakes at the proper height of the finished wall and use it as a guide during construction.

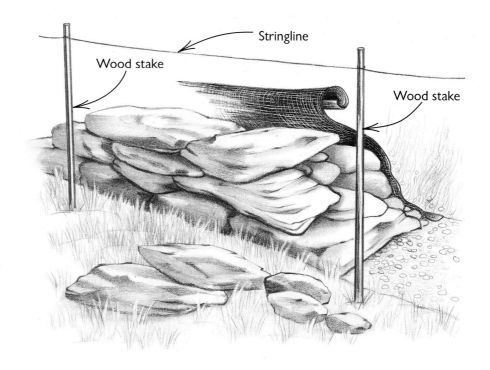

Stringline

Wood stake

Wood stake

CUTTING STONE

Sometimes you need to chisel away stone to make the pieces fit together.

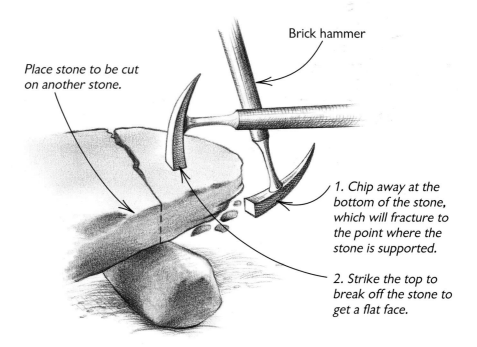

Brick hammer

Place stone to be cut on another stone.

1. Chip away at the bottom of the stone, which will fracture to the point where the stone is supported.

2. Strike the top to break off the stone to get a flat face.

Corners and ends should be square, and capstones should stretch the entire width of the wall, fitting perfectly with the ones beside them.

and washed gravel, but leave about 6 in. to 12 in. of space between the stones and the backfill. Place plastic filter fabric against the stones and fill the space with ¾-in. washed gravel. The inherent spaces in a dry-laid wall will serve as weep holes to ease drainage, but without the filter fabric, silt and soil would plug the holes and cause the wall to lose integrity. Use flat, small stones as shims on the face of the wall to keep the stones straight within the wall and to fill gaps.

Corners and ends should be square (see the photo above), and you should pick from the square stones you set aside earlier. If you don't have a lot of 90° stones, square up some stones with a hammer and chisel or with a brick hammer.

You may step the wall up or down to follow a slope (see the photo on the facing page), keeping the step square and finished down to the next level of capping.

Cap the wall with large, flat stones that stretch the entire width of the wall and fit perfectly with the ones

beside them. You may want to adhere the capstones to the top layer of wall with adhesive. I think a wall isn't a good wall if you can't sit or walk on it, and the adhesive will keep the capstones in place.

The top of the gravel backfill should stop 4 in. from the top of the wall, and the rest of the space should be topsoil so that grass can be planted right up to the wall. If a planting bed will grace the top of the wall, go ahead and fill with gravel to the top, and start the plantings beyond the gravel, at least 1 ft. away. This is far enough to allow for proper drainage behind

Step a wall to follow a slope or to make returns on stairways, keeping the steps square and finished looking on all sides.

the wall, yet close enough to allow plants to hang over or cover the top of the wall, if desired.

Stonework requires skill and patience. My landscape crews have been known to wander frustrated among the stones, looking for the perfect fit. Try a small wall first to see if you have the knack and the patience. It is such a large undertaking that unless you are prepared to give up most every weekend of the summer, it may be worthwhile to hire a contractor to build the wall. You can help by preparing the base, moving the stones around, and doing the cleanup, backfilling, and planting. This is one job that cannot be rushed, and you don't want to do it twice if it falls down because the base is too small or the rocks don't fit together well. It is also one job that looks obviously amateurish if not done by a craftsman.

CHAPTER 6

Walkways, Patios, and Decks

When you drew your landscape plan in Chapter 4, I told you to be creative when designing any walkways, patios, or decks that would be included in your landscape. I encouraged you to employ curves wherever possible to make these structures flow with the landscape and to provide interesting planting spaces.

The secondary walkways here are narrower than the main walkway and fade into the landscape.

Years ago, you may have thought I was crazy, telling you to build a curved walkway, patio, or deck. The amount of time and the difficulty of building curved structures would have been out of the question—and budget—of most people. But today, we no longer have to follow the straight and narrow, as many of our parents did. Modern building technology has provided us with the materials and techniques to build walkways, patios, and decks to almost any shape we want at little or no extra expense. Perhaps the best thing about these building systems is that they are simple enough that almost any homeowner can use them. All it takes are some rented tools, some know-how, and a willing partner.

DESIGNING WALKWAYS AND PATIOS

A well-designed walkway or patio is one that integrates form with function. Walkways and patios should not only be attractive, but they also must accommodate people and should be in keeping with the architecture of the house and your style of living. Here are some specific design criteria to consider as you plan walkways and patios.

Walkways
The front entry of your home should suit your family's needs and create a positive, lasting first impression with your guests. The walkway is the most important

element of the front entry, and it should be the focal point that all the other landscape components are built around.

A walkway should be at least 4 ft. wide to allow two people to walk comfortably side by side. Secondary walkways may be narrower (see the photo above). In fact, if two doors are on the front of the house, the walkway to a secondary entrance should fade into the landscape and be a bit narrower than the main walkway, which will direct guests naturally toward the front door. This can be accomplished by building the secondary walkway out of a different material than the main walkway, by making it meander a bit, or by concealing the

TOO MANY STEPS

To avoid having too many steps at one spot, as in the example shown here, regrade the yard so you can make the steps shorter (see the photo below). Regrading will also hide the ugly exposed foundation.

A retaining wall on the right side of the house retains the soil level, and soil added to the front yard hides the foundation. Now the foundation is covered, and only a few steps are needed to reach the front door.

entrance to the walkway with a vertical plant, such as an evergreen.

A curved walkway is more graceful than a straight one and allows for adjacent planting beds to create a natural-looking edge. A straight walkway mimics the geometry of the house and offers no relief from the flat planes of the walls. Sweeping the walkway away from the walls allows your guests a perspective view of the whole landscape and house facade as they approach the entry. Also, splaying the walkway at the street or driveway where it originates serves as an invitation to your guests.

A walkway should be level except for proper grading to shed water. If there is a slope in the yard, steps should be incorporated in the walkway to eliminate it, but not all of the steps should be at the house. Actually, the house does not look "planted" in the ground if there are several steps at the door and too much foundation is revealed, as shown in the drawing at left. It's better to backfill to within 4 in. of the siding, then add two or three steps to get to the walkway, as shown in the photo at left.

With a long slope, plan one step down from the threshold onto a large landing, at least 4 ft. to 5 ft. out from the door. From the landing, add two or three more steps of equal rise (6 in. to 8 in.) to the walkway. Add more steps and landings farther down the walkway as needed. Grading may have to be done to create this situation, but it will be easier to climb two or three small sets of steps with long landings in between than one long set of steps, and it will look better (see the top photo on the facing page).

In a yard with a long sloped area, incorporate steps with long landings into the walkway. This makes the climb more gradual and easier to negotiate than climbing several steps in one area.

Patios

Because I talked a lot about designing patios in Chapter 4, I'm not going to go into great detail here. Instead, I just want to remind you of a few things. As I mentioned, patios can be round, oval, kidney-shaped, or free form. A curved patio takes advantage of every foot of space available, unlike a square or rectangle with unusable corners. It also makes it easy to be creative with planting beds and walkways.

A patio can also have more than one level to accommodate a sloping site (see the photo at right). This allows you to create separate nooks for dining, hot tubs, or any number of activities.

A free-form patio on two levels creates areas for different uses and disguises a long, gradual slope.

When designing a patio, you should consider the average number of guests you usually entertain and allow space for them. You should also allow space for furniture—not forgetting the barbecue—and have a sense of the degree of formality you want. What you figure here will determine the size patio you need (the same design criteria are applied to wooden decks, which I'll discuss later).

CHOOSING MATERIALS FOR WALKWAYS AND PATIOS

A meandering path through the woods is best made of bark mulch or gravel, but walkways need a more substantial surface. A front walkway must provide secure footing to accommodate people of all sizes and ages, including toddling young children and less than surefooted elderly people, and must be easily cleared of snow, ice, and rain, especially if it is to be used often.

There are many materials to choose from for a walkway or patio. I have chosen to discuss a representative group of surfaces that you can install, or at least help install, because they do not need deep concrete footings and major equipment. These include poured concrete, bluestone, field-stone, bricks, and concrete pavers.

Which you choose will depend on your color choices, on the design, and, of course, on your budget.

Poured concrete

Poured concrete is the least-expensive solid surface. With poured concrete, it's possible to curve the walkway or patio, color it, and give it texture by stamping it. (Stamping is the process of imprinting shapes and colors in the concrete to make it look like natural stone or pavers.) Some stamped surfaces are so well done that it is very hard to tell that the material is really concrete.

Any custom work will, of course, raise the price of the job. If you plan on having the concrete

This wide bluestone walkway blends with nature's colors and the colors of the house. It is pulled away from the house to allow for planting beds.

stamped to look like concrete pavers, it's worthwhile to check the price of having real pavers installed. You might discover that the real thing is less expensive than the look-alike.

If you have no experience pouring concrete, it's a good idea to hire a professional. To save money, ask the contractor if you can work with him. He may allow you to design the shape of the walkway or patio and prepare the base according to his specifications, which will cut back on costs considerably. Then all the concrete contractor will need to do is form, pour, and level the concrete, and add color or texture if you desire them.

Bluestone

Bluestone can be laid on a proper base of dry materials for a contemporary, natural walkway or patio that blends with nature's colors (see the photo on the facing page). The material can be cut in squares or rectangles, randomly edged, and even sawn into curves.

Most stone suppliers import bluestone from quarries in eastern states, including New York and Pennsylvania. Bluestone is bought in 6-in. increments, in squares and rectangles of varying sizes, and you can request exactly how many of what sizes you want. I've used pieces up to 4 ft. in length for stair treads. In general, the larger the piece, the greater the cost and the more difficult it is to handle. I normally use pieces up to 3 ft. for a main walkway or patio.

Bluestone can be mixed with other materials as an edging. For instance, the body of the patio or walkway can be brick, with a 6-in.- to 12-in.-wide bluestone edging for a finishing touch. Bluestone can also be used as stepping stones for a secondary walkway. Choose pieces for stepping stones that are at least 1 in. thick and 18 in. to 24 in. long or wide so that they will be heavy enough to stay in place.

Plan the pattern you want beforehand (see the drawings below) so that you can order pieces cut to size. Using square stones all the same size will give a checkerboard effect. You can make a symmetrical pattern using two or three different-size pieces, which creates a somewhat formal look. I like to create a random pattern using different-size stones, which creates a relaxed look.

Fieldstone

Fieldstone, which is a flat, quarried natural stone, makes a rustic,

LAYING OUT BLUESTONE

Checkerboard

Symmetrical

Random

A rustic fieldstone patio has space between the stones for low ground covers like creeping thyme.

country walkway. Personally, I feel it is not the best choice for a main walkway or patio because of its uneven surface. A tripping guest or a rocking table will cure your doubt. If you have access to a quarry and can be sure you will receive perfect stones, fieldstone may be fine.

Again, I recommend using stone that is indigenous to your area to reinforce and integrate with the surrounding environment. In the East and Midwest, grays and gray-blues will blend well and recede from your eye, so that your plantings and other accents will be the focal points of the yard. In the

Southwest and West, pink sandstone will mix well with adobe and sun-drenched succulents and cacti.

Building with fieldstone is similar to making a jigsaw puzzle because the pieces are not cut exactly square or rectangular, and it is hard to meet the edges as closely as you may want, which is another factor to consider for unsteady walkers and spike-heeled shoe wearers. I recommend using stone dust (very coarsely ground rock) in between the stones, which packs and can set up almost as well as concrete after several soakings from rain. Some people opt for grass or low-growing ground covers between the stones

(see the photo above), which looks charming and informal, but shoveling and maintaining the walkway or patio will be difficult at best.

Bricks

Bricks offer a smooth, close-knit, colorful alternative to poured concrete. Typical building bricks or old bricks will be okay for a pathway through a garden, but bricks used in maintained walkways and patios will crumble and deteriorate over time, especially in cold climates, where freezing-and-thawing cycles heave the ground and crack the bricks. A better alternative is to use paving bricks, which are made of clay with additives to help them withstand

Paving bricks for outdoor use will withstand freezing-and-thawing cycles.

freezing-and-thawing cycles and which will stand up better to nature (see the photo at left). Paving bricks are a bit more expensive than building bricks.

You must not run heavy machinery over any kind of brick, and you must lay an adequate base beneath the bricks for a smooth, long-lasting result. Rectangular bricks may be laid in many patterns (see the drawings below), the most popular being running bond, basketweave, and herringbone. Depending on the size of your patio or walkway, installing bricks can be labor intensive and time-consuming.

Precast concrete pavers

Precast concrete pavers are by far more durable and reliable than building or paving bricks. They are uniform in size, come in many colors and shapes, can be mixed and matched, and some can even withstand the weight of a car.

LAYING OUT BRICK

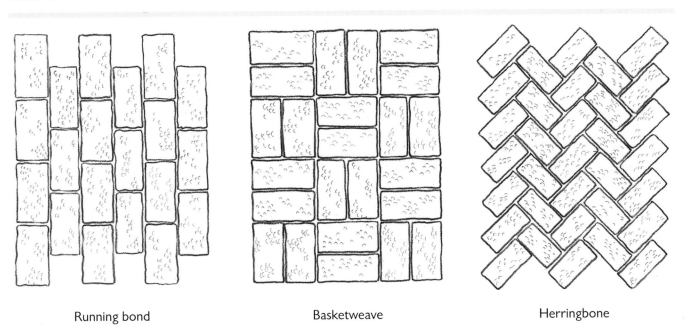

Running bond   Basketweave   Herringbone

Some precast concrete pavers are shaped to make a perfect circle without gaps.

Each paver edge is designed to act like an expansion joint, allowing fluctuations from freezing and thawing without paver movement. With proper base preparation, installation, and edging, concrete pavers are appropriate for country and city properties and can be used to create any level of formality or informality you can imagine. One paver design is specifically shaped to create curves and circles without gaps (see the photo above).

I have used precast concrete pavers for walkways, patios, driveways, and even shopping-mall sidewalks. Wherever you use them, they should be installed on a dry base and edged with an underground system so that driveways, grass, and planting beds meet the pavers with a smooth transition.

INSTALLING A DRY-LAID WALKWAY OR PATIO

In my early days of landscaping, before precast concrete pavers made the scene, I experimented with base preparation for dry-laid systems, usually overdoing it with too much handwork, too much sand, or too deep a base. Although methods may continue to evolve as new materials are introduced and

used, I believe there are certain keys to proper dry-laid construction that will never change, and to be successful, you must not cut corners or vary too much from these instructions, regardless of the surface material being used.

The tools for this job (see the left photo on the facing page) include a wheelbarrow, shovels, rakes, a diamond-bladed dry or wet saw, sledgehammer, pick ax, plate compactor, some straight 2x4s for a screed-board setup, and, depending on the size of the job, a skid-steer loader.

Tools for patio and walkway construction include, from left to right: sledgehammer, wheelbarrow, rake, shovel, wet saw, plate compactor, pick ax, and skid-steer loader.

A plate compactor is used to compact the base material properly. Run it over the surface at intervals as you fill the excavation.

Digging the hole

First and foremost, you must dig a hole with a uniform depth of 8 in. to 12 in.—lean toward 12 in. if you live in a really cold area (one that's colder than Zone 6). The job will be easier with a skid-steer loader than with a hand shovel, although there will be handwork along the edges. The hole should be at least 6 in. wider than the finished size to allow for installation of the edging material.

You must decide which way you want water to drain, and then with a grading rake, grade the bottom of the hole accordingly. Sometimes the water will need to be shed in more than one direction, for instance, to the sides as well as along the length of a walkway (see the drawing at right). A pitch of 1 in. in 8 ft. should be sufficient and will be imperceptible to the eye (for more on grading, see Chapter 1). Of course, make sure the water is directed away from the house. As you work, check the grade frequently.

The base at the bottom of the hole must be well compacted. A well-graded, smooth base will translate into a smooth, continuous surface on the top. A plate compactor is really the only tool that will do the job as thoroughly as it needs to be done (see the right photo above). A plate compactor can be rented, and except for removing it from the trunk and putting it back in, it is really quite easy to operate. It is a tool you will use over and over again in the course of this project.

Adding gravel

Next, fill the hole with ¾-in. gravel, leaving 1 in. at the top for coarse sand (for bricks or precast concrete pavers) or stone dust (for bluestone or fieldstone) and enough space to accommodate the surface material

MOVING WATER OFF A WALKWAY

A curved walkway may have to be pitched (1 in. in 8 ft.) in two or more directions to move water efficiently.

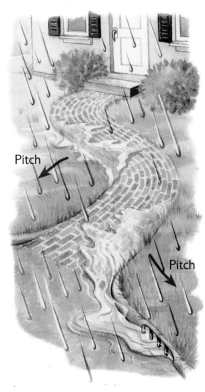

Pitch

Pitch

Good-packing base material contains ¾-in. gravel mixed with smaller stone and stone dust (bottom). Stone dust is used as a bed for bluestone or fieldstone (top left). Coarse sand beds brick and concrete pavers (top right).

A screed board lies on two 2x4 rails. The rails should be parallel to each other, and the 2-in. edges should be flush with the gravel. The screed board is dragged across the rails to achieve a level, smooth surface.

you are using (simply measure the thickness of the material and leave that much space).

Do not use washed peastone; the gravel should be of different aggregate sizes up to ¾ in. and should include clean stone dust that's free of other debris (see the top photo at left). This type of mix will compact well. Add it in layers and compact with the plate compactor after each one—if not after each one, at least on two layers before you are through backfilling with the gravel. Check the grade frequently as you backfill and compact.

After backfilling to the correct height, smooth the surface with a screed board made from a straight 2x4 (reject any twisted wood). Cut the length to the exact width of the walkway or to a manageable length for a patio.

Cut two other 2x4s to the same length and bury them as far apart as the width of the walkway or as far apart as the length of the screed board for a patio. The screed board will ride on these 2x4 rails. The rails should be parallel to each other, and the 2-in. edges should be flush with the gravel (see the bottom photo at left). Depending on which direction you have chosen to shed water, one end or side might be higher than the other.

Next, kneel between the rails, lay the screed board across them, and drag it toward you, scraping it for the length of the rails. Repeat, if necessary, to fill any low areas as you go, or add more gravel and repeat, compact again, and screed again until the surface is perfectly flush with the rails. Then remove the rails, fill the holes left behind, tamp them with a hand tamper, and move the rails to the next un-screeded area. Continue screeding until the entire area has been done.

Adding sand or stone dust

Once you've completed the gravel backfilling process, you're ready to add sand or stone dust. First, make a set of rails out of 1-in.-dia. PVC pipes. Lay them on top of the gravel subsurface in the same position as the wood rails. Add about 1 in. of coarse sand, not fine sandbox sand, on top of the gravel. Compact with the plate compactor. Screed again, removing any excess sand and adding sand if an area is too low. Whenever you add sand, you will need to compact and screed again until all you are doing is removing excess sand. Then remove the pipes, fill the gaps left by them, tamp with the hand tamper, and move the pipes to the next area until the entire surface is smooth and ready for the surface material. The 1-in. pipes will leave a base with perfect thickness.

For bluestone, it is also acceptable and may be preferable to use stone dust, sometimes called rock fines, as the bedding material instead of sand. Because bluestone is a natural material, its thickness may vary slightly, needing a bedding material like stone dust that can be slightly

Black PVC edging is spiked in and sits below grade so that it isn't visible when the surface material of the walkway or patio is in place.

adjusted as the stones are leveled each one with the next. If you use stone dust, follow the base preparation for bricks and pavers. Fieldstone can be bedded in stone dust in the same fashion, but it will be necessary to dig out for each stone to accommodate the variable faces and depths.

Placing the surface material

Some edgings are installed first. I prefer the type made of PVC plastic that slips under the outside bricks and anchors in the ground with spiked flanges (see the photo on p. 71). It comes in flexible material for curves or stiff PVC for straight lengths. The edging is completely invisible once the edges of the walkway or patio have been backfilled. Follow the manufacturer's instructions for installing the edging.

The final step is to lay the surface material in the desired pattern, keeping the joints as tight as possible. Place only full-size pieces for now, leaving spaces for the pieces to be cut. After you've placed all the full-size pieces, begin cutting the others to size and installing them.

To cut stones, bricks, or pavers, you'll need to use a diamond-bladed wet or dry saw. It is easiest to hold the piece over its location, score it with a sharp nail or mark it with a pencil, as shown in the photo at left, and then cut along the line. If anything, it's best to cut the piece too large and trim it back if it doesn't fit.

After all the pieces have been installed, spread dry sand on top. For bricks, sweep it into the cracks. For concrete pavers, run the plate compactor on top of the surface to vibrate the sand into the joints. For stones with stone dust as the bedding, sweep dry stone dust into the joints. When grass or ground covers will be used between the stones, sweep topsoil into the joints and plant in them. Finally, backfill the outside of the edging with topsoil, right up to the surface material, in preparation for lawn or garden installation.

Hold the paver (or whatever surface material you use) over its location and mark the size on its edge. Then cut it with a dry or wet saw.

This curved, multilevel deck softens the straight geometry of the house and fits a contemporary setting. The deck flows naturally into the planting bed at right, tying the deck to the earth.

DESIGNING DECKS

Many people hire professionals to design and build decks for them. And this is a good idea for people who don't have carpentry experience. But even if you are hiring a professional to do the job, you don't have to stand idly by during the design stage. It's your yard and your deck, and so you should be very involved with the design. Many of the considerations that go into patio design apply here as well (see pp. 63-64). Make sure you have enough room for your family, friends, and any furniture (don't forget the barbecue), and make sure the deck fits the setting.

Many wooden decks are unimaginative, geometrical shapes and look as if they were just scabbed onto the house. But it doesn't have to be that way. There are many ways to spice up the design and to make it unique.

To tie the deck to the landscape, for instance, you can curve it or make it multilevel. A curved deck has soft edges that blend well with the landscape, and a multilevel deck works well on a sloped lot. Or you can use planting boxes to add life to the design and to bring the landscape closer to the house.

To make a deck more functional, add benches and other built-in furniture. You can even put a shade structure over the deck to provide a cool area for family and guests during the hot summer months. A shade structure is also a perfect place to plant climbing vines.

As for lumber, don't feel that you must use only pressure-treated wood. Woods like greenheart, cedar, or redwood, although expensive, are an attractive alternative to the dull-green look of pressure-treated lumber. Plus they are rot resistant and weather over time to a natural gray finish that blends with the landscape. If you don't have a large budget for lumber, use a less-expensive alternative, such as Douglas fir and paint or stain it (but use pressure-treated lumber for parts that contact the ground).

Although small, this deck has a lot of features. The shade structure covers only part of the deck so that sun lovers can soak up the rays while those looking for a cool spot can find it on the built-in benches. The painting scheme ties the deck to the house, and the potted plants add color and life.

Planting boxes bring the landscape to the back door of the house. They are great for herbs and spices, especially if the deck is near the kitchen. This box is snuggled into the corner of the deck, and the plants contrast with the color of the redwood. The built-in benches near the plants allow people to get close to the landscape without leaving their seats.

Painting the deck can add life and interest to the design and can help the deck blend in with both the house and the yard.

Probably the biggest limiting factor in the design is the budget. Obviously, the more custom touches you put into the deck, the more money you will spend. You'll have to work with your contractor so that you stay within the budget, which may mean compromising on a few issues. But you may be able to step in to help in certain areas to save money. For instance, if you pour the footings or do the finish work yourself, you may be able to save enough money to hold onto a unique design element that would otherwise have been tossed due to budget constraints (for more on hiring and working with a professional, see Chapter 12).

On the previous page and on these two pages, you can see a sampling of decks with attractive, unique designs. Feel free to use these photos for inspiration as you design your deck. If you want more detailed instructions on deck construction, a good place to start is by reading *Building and Designing Decks* by Scott Schuttner (see Further Reading on p. 161).

The redwood on this deck matches the brick siding of the house. The irregular shape of the deck takes best advantage of the space available and provides both sunny and shady nooks. Without obtrusive railings on the near side, the deck steps naturally into the landscape.

A deck doesn't have to be attached to a house. This detached deck is tucked into the shoreline to take advantage of the spectacular waterfront view. The surrounding trees provide a natural screen from the sun.

CHAPTER 7

Fences

Regardless of where you live—whether in an urban, suburban, or country setting—a fence can be an effective way to enhance your landscape design. But drive down any street, and you'll see yards with fences just plopped down simply to delineate property lines. The fences were chosen and installed without regard to how they would fit into the yard, so they often don't work with the landscape and don't provide any aesthetic benefit to the property.

A privacy fence doesn't have to be solid and boring like a traditional wooden stockade fence. This lattice fence with decorative finials is an effective privacy fence.

FUNCTION AND AESTHETICS

Ultimately, function will dictate the size and type of fence you choose. For instance, a high, solid fence (6 ft. to 8 ft. tall) can be used not only to delineate property but also to make a yard more private by blocking out neighboring yards. It can also effectively block out wind and noise (see the photo above). A fence of medium height (4 ft. to 5 ft. tall), open or solid style, can be used to delineate areas on the property, to keep in a dog, to make a play area in the yard for the kids, to surround a pool, to protect a vegetable garden from animals, or

to shield an unsightly feature in the yard, such as a compost bin or an animal pen (see the left photo on p. 78). And a low fence (2 ft. to 3 ft. tall) can be used to support vines and tall perennials or to enhance a walkway, patio, or entry of a house (see the right photo on p. 78).

But a fence chosen for a specific function should work with the landscape design. With the limited fence materials and styles of the past, this was not always easy or cost effective to accomplish. But with advancements in today's building technology and materials, there's no reason why you can't

find a fence option that will work well with your landscape. The possibilities are almost limitless.

You can even dress up a fence by adding plantings near it or on it to make the fence blend naturally with the landscape. For instance, you can cover a fence with climbing vines, espalier a tree on it, or plant shrubs in front of it. For an even more natural look, and if you have a lot of space to play with, an effective alternative to a traditional fence is a living fence, in which plantings are substituted for man-made fence materials. This can be done with hedgerows or strategically placed informal plantings.

A fence can delineate yard areas, such as the pool area above, or it can be ornamental and functional. For instance, the fence at right delineates the front yard of the house and supports tall perennials.

TRADITIONAL FENCES WITH A TWIST

Finding a functional fence that will blend into the landscape does not mean you have to spend big bucks to have a fence custom-designed and built for your yard. You can now buy traditional fence designs that will accommodate most any budget and that will fit most any landscape plan. Another option is to customize one of these designs to suit your tastes.

You'll need to spend some time at your local fence supplier looking at what options will be most functional and most attractive for your situation. As with any home project, budget will be paramount,

so pick the best option for the money. Here are a few ideas to get you started.

Chain link

Chain link is one of the most common types of fences around. It is available in tall or short heights and lasts a long time if properly installed. Chain-link fences, although extremely functional, are not attractive (I think they're downright ugly), so I don't usually recommend them. More often than not, a chain-link fence will make your yard look more like an industrial site than a home. One good thing about chain link is that it is easy to dress up with climbing vines (see the top photo on p. 89).

Privacy

A privacy fence is tall (at least 6 ft.) and provides a solid barrier to noise, wind, and neighbors. A wooden stockade fence is the traditional style. A drawback to stockade fences is that they look pretty much the same, and there are not many ways to customize them or make them attractive, besides adding some paint. But today you don't have to use stockade as a privacy fence if you don't want to.

Today's privacy fences have been much improved in terms of the attractive designs available. Now you don't have to hide a privacy fence behind trees or bushes because of its mundane, unattractive look. Instead, you can use it as a decorative element in the yard.

Mix-and-match fence panels make a privacy fence more attractive and versatile. This style is solid on the bottom with open spindles on top and has a prominent role in the yard.

There are two common styles of modern privacy fences—solid and open. Solid styles include traditional stockade, board and batten, overlapping vertical panels, and horizontal clapboard. Open styles have spindles (vertical slats or bars) or latticework attached between the rails of the fence.

One thing that's especially appealing about modern privacy fences is that some designs allow you to mix and match styles in one 6-ft.-tall fence. For instance, I like to use a 5-ft.-tall solid board-and-batten section topped with a 1-ft.-tall section of open spindles (see the photo above), which adds a touch of elegance to the fence. Or you can place 3 ft. of open fencing on top of 3 ft. of solid fencing to make the fence less imposing and to allow you to see through part of it.

Fence sections are available in different widths to accommodate corners and other special situations. A privacy fence can be stained or painted to blend (or contrast, if you prefer) with the landscape and house.

You should consult with your fence dealer to find out what's out there. With all the designs available, finding a privacy fence that fits in with your yard, your budget, and your home's architecture should be a cinch.

Wrought iron

The traditional wrought-iron fence has been used over the years as an elegant but simple method of delineating a yard. The spindles are close enough to prevent children and some animals from passing through the fence but are far enough apart and slender enough to be unobtrusive to the view beyond.

There are two big drawbacks of a traditional wrought-iron fence. First, it is expensive. Second, over time, the iron will begin to rust, and so regular sanding and painting are required for upkeep.

But with improved manufacturing techniques, you can get the look of wrought iron for a fraction of

This fence looks like real wrought iron, but it's actually made of aluminum, which is less expensive and easier to maintain than the real thing.

A picket fence can be dressed up with sculpted finials and pickets, and perennial planting beds in front hide gaps between the earth and the slats.

the price. Fence designs from the Victorian age—as well as a multitude of other designs—can now be made with aluminum (see the top photo at left), which is far less expensive, lighter, and easier to maintain than real wrought iron. Aluminum does not rust and does not need painting. Fence sections are typically 4 ft. wide, with heights of 2 ft. to 6 ft., and are available with a white or black finish.

Picket

A picket fence is a traditional method of delineating a yard and works well to keep children and some animals in—or out—of a yard or an area in the yard. When most folks think of a picket fence, however, they imagine the stereotypical home with the ordinary white picket fence.

But I tell clients considering a picket fence to stray from the ordinary. Dress up the fence: Place finials on top of the posts, sculpt a design into the pickets (the vertical slats), vary the height of the sections, or paint the fence a color other than white.

You can buy stock finials for the posts at lumberyards and fence suppliers, or you can create your own design and either make them yourself (if you're handy in the woodshop) or have them custom made. Be aware that custom woodwork will cost more than stock material.

If you don't like the look of regular pickets, change them (see the bottom photo at left). Make them spoon shaped or even animal shaped. George Washington didn't settle for ordinary pickets at Mount Vernon. He had quails carved into the top of each picket.

If you are building the fence yourself, you can ensure exact reproduction of the design by drawing it at the top of one picket, and cutting out the shape with a jigsaw. Then you can use that picket as a template to make the rest identical.

A picket fence can be made less ordinary by building it in a rhythmic pattern of waves (see the photo on p. 76), alternating between tall and shorter sections. A colleague of mine designed a courtyard for a cottage where several of the picket panels were 4 ft. tall and others were 6 ft. tall. This served two purposes: to shield approaching headlights at strategic points and to create a very striking effect that mingled well with the 19th-century architecture of the cottage.

For a more colorful effect and to contrast with the color of the fencing, cover the fence with a flowering vine, or plant perennials around it. For instance, I covered a white picket fence with rambling pink roses to create a romantic look for one client.

Post-and-rail

A post-and-rail fence is a simple way to delineate a property, and it has often been used on farms to corral livestock. However, because of the large openings between rails, a post-and-rail fence is not typically used as a barrier to prevent children from entering a pool area unsupervised or from leaving a play area.

A SAFE POST-AND-RAIL FENCE

A post-and-rail fence can be an effective barrier around a pool or play yard when it's covered with hardware cloth. The hardware cloth is also a perfect base on which to grow climbing vines to make the fence more natural looking.

CLIMBING VINES

Here's a sampling of a few climbing vines that work well for dressing up an ordinary fence. They will also work well on shade structures, such as trellises and arbors.

• For unusual-colored foliage, try *Actinidia Kolomikta* (hardy kiwi). It has leaves with pink and white blotches, and small fragrant, white flowers in spring, followed by greenish yellow kiwi fruit (photo 1). The cultivar 'Arctic Beauty' is especially hardy, surviving in Zone 5 climates.

• With its huge leaves and interesting, U-shaped yellow flowers, *Aristolochia durior* (Dutchman's pipe) creates a dense privacy and shade cover (photo 2).

• Tropical gardeners can enjoy *Bougainvillea* with showy red, purple, yellow, or pink flower bracts (photo 3).

• *Campsis radicans* (trumpet creeper) is vigorous with tubular red flowers (photo 4) and thrives in sunny locations.

• Many cultivars of *Hedera Helix* (evergreen ivy) are suited to shady sites. But for more interest, try 'Gold Heart', which has white veins (photo 5), 'Atropurpurea' with purplish leaves and light-green veins, 'Buttercup' or 'Gold Heart' with creamy golden variegation, and 'Parsley Crested' with crinkled foliage. 'Thorndale', with glossy green leaves and white veins, is one of the hardiest cultivars of these Zone 6 vines.

• *Humulus Lupulus* 'Aureus' (yellow hops) has large lime-green leaves that rapidly cover a fence (photo 6).

• *Hydrangea anomala petiolaris* (climbing hydrangea) bears large clusters of white flowers during the summer and has golden yellow fall color (photo 7).

• There are several honeysuckles to try, but *Lonicera Heckrottii* (goldflame honeysuckle) blooms for a long time with clusters of purple and yellow flowers (photo 8). *L. sempervirens* (evergreen trumpet honeysuckle) produces long tubes of orange-red flowers with yellow insides and orange-red fruit.

• Deciduous *Parthenocissus tricuspidata* (Boston ivy) has brilliant orange and red fall foliage (photo 9).

• *Wisteria floribunda* and *W. sinensis* (old-fashioned wisteria) have long, drooping clusters of white, purple, or pink flowers (photo 10).

• *Polygonum Aubertii* (silver lace vine) makes a dense screen and provides clusters of tiny white flowers in late summer (photo 11).

• For outstanding flowers and red rose hip fruit, choose *Rosa setigera* (climbing rose) (photo 12). Try 'Blaze' with red flowers, 'Don Juan' with profuse, fragrant, maroon flowers that bloom again, 'New Dawn' with pale pink blooms, and 'Golden Showers' with yellow flowers.

7

8

9

10

11

12

But one way to make a post-and-rail fence more of a barrier is to stretch hardware cloth across the sections and staple it to the posts. Hardware cloth is a sturdy, thick wire mesh that comes plain or coated with plastic (green is a common color) to make it less noticeable. It can be found at most hardware stores or home centers.

Hardware cloth makes the fencing an effective enclosure device. Plus the cloth is unobtrusive, so you can see views beyond, if that's what you want. But if you don't want to see the cloth at all and don't care if your views are blocked, the cloth also provides a perfect opportunity to cover the fencing with climbing vines (for a list of climbing vines, see pp. 82-83), which will hide the mesh and make the fencing blend into the landscape.

Unfortunately, a traditional wood post-and-rail fence needs to be painted annually. But thanks to modern building materials, you can now buy post-and-rail fences made of PVC plastic, which never needs to be painted. I challenge anyone to tell the difference between a PVC fence and a wood fence without

A PVC post-and-rail fence looks like real wood, but it's easier to maintain because it doesn't need painting. This fence in Vermont has matching stone pillars at every other section to add a touch of formality to its bucolic setting.

touching it. The disadvantage to a PVC fence is its cost, which is 50% to 75% more than the cost of a wood post-and-rail fence.

The PVC post-and-rail fence was developed in Saratoga, New York, for the horse industry because the horses kept chewing up the wood rails and posts. But they won't chew through the plastic. The only maintenance involved with a PVC post-and-rail fence is an annual cleaning with a hose.

I installed a PVC post-and-rail fence in the yard of a stone-faced home in rural Vermont. To tie the fence into the house and to add a touch of formality, I built matching stone pillars as posts at every other section (see the photo on the facing page). The rails slide into premade holes in the pillars for an uninterrupted enclosure. Along with the pillars, flowering shrubs and perennials adorn the fence, breaking up the monotony of acres of white rails.

INSTALLATION

As I have mentioned, a fence should not only perform a function, but it should also look good in its setting while doing so. To achieve both of these goals, care must be taken in the installation. Remember, the fence will be subject to abuse: It must stand up to both people and nature, with nature being the tougher of the two.

People will be passing through gates, they could lean or sit on the fence, and there'll be an occasional bump with a lawn mower or other tool, or even a toy. Mother Nature will be ruthless, soaking the fence with rain, baking it with sun, heaving the earth beneath it during freeze-and-thaw cycles, and subjecting the fence to strong winds.

Because of these factors, you can't take shortcuts during the installation—you can't cheat. If you do, you'll find yourself spending a lot of time repairing fence sections because of premature wear.

A fence installation can be difficult, so I often recommend that homeowners hire professionals to do the job. But if you are handy with tools and are willing to do the job the right way, here are the basic steps to a fence installation. These instructions should help any installation go smoothly. But the fence manufacturer or dealer should provide you with instructions specific to the fence design you have chosen.

Tools and materials
The first step is to gather all the tools and materials needed for the installation. At the very least, you will need a carpenter's level, a tape measure, and a post-hole digger or gas-powered auger—available at rental centers (see the photo on p. 86). The gas-powered auger will be especially handy if you have to dig a lot of post holes. You may need other tools specific to the type of fence you are installing. The instructions or fence dealer should give you a list. Along with the tools, you'll need a helper or two.

If you are installing a wooden fence, make sure the posts, or any other wood parts that contact the ground, are pressure treated or made of rot-resistant woods like cedar, greenheart, or redwood. Do not cut the ends of pressure-treated lumber that contact the ground, or you will render it vulnerable to insects and rot, regardless of what the manufacturer claims. Also, use galvanized nails because they won't rust and cause stains, and paint or stain any parts of the fence that are not naturally or otherwise protected from the elements. It is perfectly acceptable to allow rot-resistant woods like cedar or redwood to attractively weather to another color.

Installing posts
Once you have all the materials and tools on hand, the installation can begin with the posts. Fence posts must be installed so that they are absolutely plumb, so you'll need to check for plumb often with a carpenter's level.

Posts should always be buried about 6 in. for every foot exposed above ground, especially when there is the threat of heaving during freeze-and-thaw cycles in colder parts of the country.

Dig the hole using a post-hole digger or a gas-powered auger. Set the post in place, and backfill to help it stand alone, but don't compact the backfill just yet. Dig the next hole, set that post, backfill, then plumb both posts.

Never dig all the holes ahead of time, even though the temptation may be great. It's entirely possible that a post will need to be adjusted slightly because you hit a hidden obstruction like a rock. If you dig all the holes ahead of time, and have to adjust the placement of one post from the previous one, you'll have to dig all the holes again.

Supporting posts

If you have buried the posts 6 in. for every foot above ground, you probably won't need additional support, besides the backfill. But if you are installing aluminum posts—which are thin and need extra support—or if you could not dig to the necessary depth to provide adequate support for a wood post because you hit bedrock or another immovable object, you'll need to pour concrete in the hole around the posts to stiffen them. If you add concrete, let the posts sit overnight before doing any more work on the fence.

If concrete isn't necessary, simply backfill the post hole with a multisized-aggregate gravel, thoroughly compacting the backfill as you go along. Compacting is important to work out air pockets, which will cause instability and heave the posts in freeze-and-thaw cycles. A flat-headed hand tamper will do the job well.

After putting in the posts, install the panels or rails according to the manufacturer's instructions.

Dealing with slope

If you are installing a fence on a slope, the job gets tricky because the posts still must be absolutely plumb, which means they will not be perpendicular to the ground. You'll need to check for plumb frequently. An easy way to install a fence on a slope is to step the panels or rails down the slope, but I

A post-hole digger is a necessary tool for a fence installation. A two-man gas-powered auger will do the job faster, though, especially if you must dig a lot of holes.

INSTALLING A FENCE ON A SLOPE

Putting in a fence on a slope is tricky because the posts must be absolutely plumb. You can step the fence down or run it along the slope.

STEP

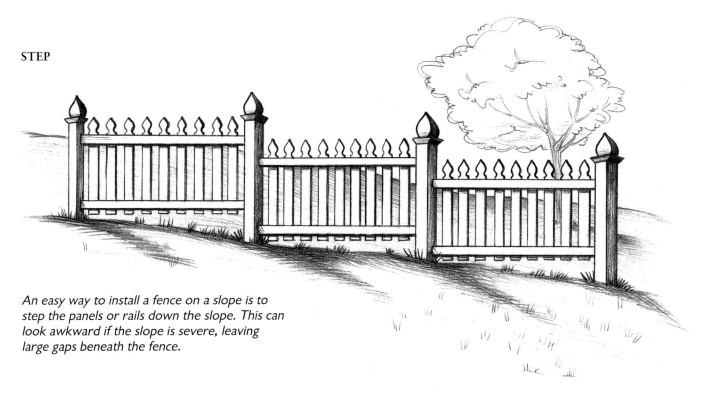

An easy way to install a fence on a slope is to step the panels or rails down the slope. This can look awkward if the slope is severe, leaving large gaps beneath the fence.

RUN

Installing the fence along the run of the slope is more natural looking. But because of the angles involved, the installation gets tricky, so you may be better off hiring a professional.

MAKING A 90° TURN

A 90° turn is easily made by creating a right triangle with string. This example shows the method for a fence with 4-ft. panels or sections.

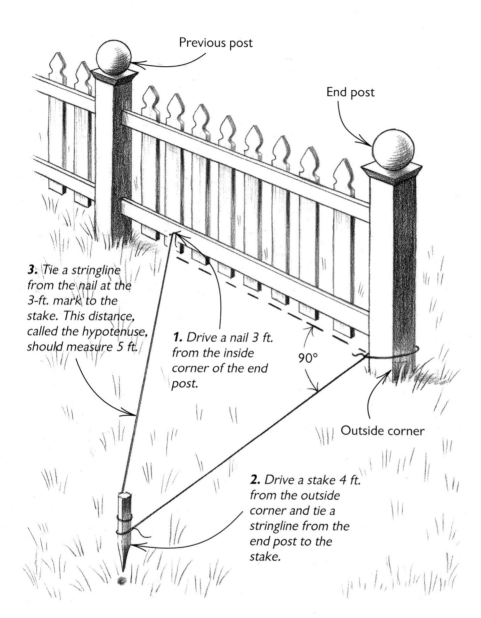

Previous post

End post

3. *Tie a stringline from the nail at the 3-ft. mark to the stake. This distance, called the hypotenuse, should measure 5 ft.*

1. *Drive a nail 3 ft. from the inside corner of the end post.*

90°

Outside corner

2. *Drive a stake 4 ft. from the outside corner and tie a stringline from the end post to the stake.*

prefer to let the fence follow a grade change in a natural manner (see the drawings on p. 87).

With a post-and-rail fence, the holes in the posts may have to be adjusted to accommodate the angled rail. Other fence styles, such as stockade, have some give to them to allow the installer to adjust the panel to fit the slope. But it's still difficult work. So if you have a sloped yard and want this look, you may be better off hiring a professional to do the job.

Turning corners

One of the hardest parts of fence installation is turning a 90° corner. But it can be simplified by recalling high-school geometry. Here's how.

For a fence with 4-ft. panels or sections, measure 3 ft. from the inside corner of the end post toward the previous post, and mark the point with a finish nail. Now measure at a right angle 4 ft. from the outside corner of the end post toward the direction the fence will be turning, and drive a stake at that point. Tie a stringline from the end post to the stake. Then tie another stringline to the nail on the panel and attach it to the stake, creating a right triangle. The hypotenuse of the triangle should measure 5 ft. When installing the next section, simply follow the stringline from the outside corner to the stake, and the corner will be square.

These dimensions can be adjusted for longer sections by equally increasing each number. For instance, if you have an 8-ft. section, measure 6 ft. toward the previous post and 8 ft. toward the stake, and the hypotenuse will be 10 ft.

An ordinary chain-link fence can be dressed up with climbing vines like English ivy (*Hedera helix*).

DRESSING UP A FENCE

You can dress up a traditional fence and make it fit more naturally with your landscape by adding climbing vines, or you can train, or espalier, a small tree or shrub to grow on the fence to dress it up (see the photos above and at right). This is a perfect solution for hiding an ugly fence, such as chain link. It also works if you no longer like the look of your fence, or if you just want something different. You can change the look without replacing the fence.

Large-leafed, vigorous climbers will create privacy, block wind, and muffle noise, while less-dense climbers will allow breezes through and provide light shade. Some vines have attractive foliage, brilliant fall

If you don't like the look of climbing vines, espalier trees on a fence. Attach a lattice to the fence for a dressed-up look and to provide support for the espaliered trees.

HINGED LATTICE FOR GROWING VINES

A hinged lattice assembly not only allows you to grow climbing vines on a fence but also allows for fence maintenance and air circulation.

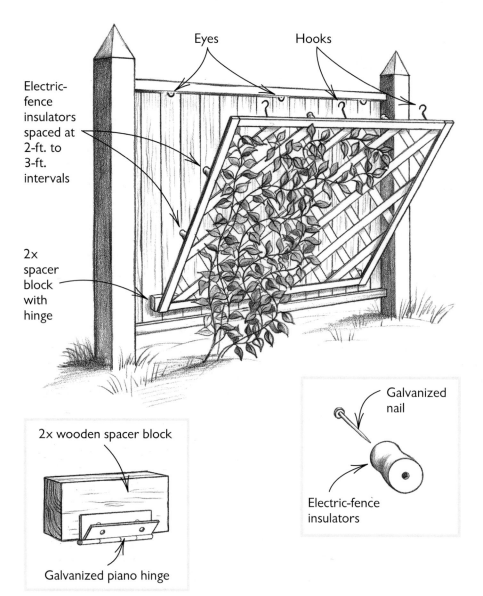

Eyes

Hooks

Electric-fence insulators spaced at 2-ft. to 3-ft. intervals

2x spacer block with hinge

2x wooden spacer block

Galvanized piano hinge

Galvanized nail

Electric-fence insulators

important that it remain accessible. It also needs ventilation so it can dry out after rainfall. One way to attach lattice but still allow for maintenance and air circulation, is to build a hinged lattice assembly. It can be built with hinges at the bottom, porcelain electric-fence insulators (available at home centers and fence suppliers) used as spacers to hold the lattice away from the fence, and hooks and eyes at the top to keep the lattice upright.

Attach galvanized, piano-type hinges at 3-ft. intervals to the bottom of the lattice and secure them to 2x wood spacer blocks on the bottom of the fence. Attach the porcelain insulators to the lattice at approximately 2 ft. to 3 ft. square intervals with galvanized or aluminum nails (you can substitute 2x blocks for the porcelain insulators). Then affix hooks to the top of the lattice and corresponding eyes to the top of the fence. When maintenance is needed, unhook the lattice and fold it down gently to avoid injuring the vines. (For a list of climbing vines that work well to dress up a fence, see pp. 82-83.)

LIVING FENCES

Although there are many man-made fence styles that could serve your needs and fit in with the landscape, nothing beats the beauty and natural look of a living fence.

A living fence may not keep people or animals in or out of a yard or areas of a yard, but it can provide plenty of privacy, wind protection, and shade, and it also works well as a noise baffle (see the drawing on the facing page).

color, or berries for seasonal interest, and others are evergreen for year-round interest.

The most difficult part of growing climbers on a fence is to get them to cling to it. On a chain-link fence, the climbers will either cling or twine around the chain link. For a post-and-rail fence or a picket

fence, attach lattice or hardware cloth between the posts to provide a place for the climbers to grow. You can even attach lattice to a wooden stockade fence for climbing vines to cling to.

A wooden stockade fence requires a lot of maintenance (such as painting and repairs), so it's

LIVING FENCE

Nothing beats the beauty and natural look of a living fence. Mix types of plants and layer them for a living fence that is functional, long-lived, and interesting to look at.

A clipped hedgerow of Canadian hemlock (*Tsuga canadensis*) creates a formal living fence.

Traditionally clipped into hedges, evergreen boxwood (*Buxus sempervirens*) adds whimsy.

A living fence could be formal, such as hedgerows cut straight or curved or a line of the same trees or shrubs. Or it could be an informal, meandering row or a mix of plant species and sizes. The possibilities are limited only by the space available and your imagination.

Planning

When planning a living fence, there are a few things you should keep in mind that don't apply to man-made fence installations.

• Locating a living fence so it straddles the property line is inviting trouble. Those cute little plants fresh from the garden center grow up to be big ones, and whatever grows onto your neighbor's property is his to prune or hack away if he so chooses. Even if it means losing a few feet of usable space, locate the plantings inside your property line.

• Allow for the potential spread of an evergreen tree or the crown of a shade tree when spacing the plants to allow enough area for natural growth and to avoid overcrowding.

• Be careful not to plant in utility or highway rights-of-way because the workers who maintain these areas are free to prune or remove whatever's in the way of electrical lines and machinery.

• To guard against an insect or disease infestation that will wipe out an entire planting of the same species, mix types of plants within the fence.

• Beware of evergreen trees that lose their lower branches with age. Members of the spruce family are particularly prone to this.

• Planting a living fence is an expensive proposition if you want instant results because mature

The smell and sight of an informal lilac (*Syringa vulgaris*) fence is intoxicating in bloom.

Old-fashioned bridalwreath (*Spiraea* × *Vanhouttei*) serves as a cascading living fence and provides early summer glory.

Crimson pygmy barberry (*Berberis Thunbergii* 'Crimson Pygmy') can be pruned to keep it tidy and has red foliage throughout the growing season.

plants are more expensive than younger ones. To get the fence started, don't hesitate to plant fast-growing, shorter-lived species like wide-spreading Russian olive (*Elaeagnus angustifolia*) or tall-growing Lombardy poplar (*Populus nigra* 'Italica'). While these grow quickly and will fill the area temporarily, you can plant younger, slower-growing, sturdier trees and shrubs. In a few years, the sturdier trees and shrubs will establish themselves and mature. When they are large enough to serve as the fence alone, you can remove the temporary plantings.

• If the fence is to serve as a wind break, avoid trees that are intolerant of wind and that will burn, such as white pine (*Pinus Strobus*) and hemlock. Instead, try Austrian pine (*Pinus nigra*) or Scotch pine (*Pinus sylvestris*) which are tougher.

• When planning a formal living fence, choose evergreens like hemlock and arborvitae, which can be planted in single-file rows or in double, staggered rows for a thicker fence. Hemlocks will grow wide and tall and will tolerate shade, but they also can be pruned into a formal shape. Arborvitae grow fast, are happy in wet areas, and are narrower in stature. They need to be planted close together to form a solid fence, but the cultivar 'Techny' is wider and slower growing and is a good choice for hedging.

• When planning an informal living fence, include layers of plantings, combining larger species like pines, firs, maples, and oaks with shrubby viburnums, lilacs, and winterberry (*Ilex verticillata*), which fill the gaps at ground level. Beneath that, plant ground covers and woodsy perennials to add another level.

Different size trees, shrubs, and perennials can be layered to create an informal, meandering living fence.

CHAPTER 8

Adding Garden Features

After a busy day, there's no better place to be than in a cozy retreat in the yard. It could be a shady nook, where you can nap in a hammock stretched between two trees, or it could be in a cool, shaded gazebo, where you can curl up in a chaise lounge with a good book. Or, perhaps, you'd prefer to find solace while sipping a cold drink near a water garden.

Shade trees provide a wonderful retreat for a hammock-bound soul.

I think it's important to create a private space in the yard. I'm not talking about the deck or patio, where you entertain a large number of people or gather with the family. I'm talking about a small area—an outdoor living room, so to speak—where you can relax alone or with a couple of friends.

Shade structures and water gardens are often chosen by people looking to create a serene nook in their yard. They can be complex or simple, but no matter what your preference, either feature requires a lot of planning. If you want to add a water garden or shade structure—or both—make sure you set aside space for them as you draw up your landscape plan (see Chapter 4).

Both shade structures and water gardens, however, require certain skills and great patience. To build a wooden shade structure, for instance, you'll need carpentry skills; for a water garden, you'll need keen design skills and a good amount of brawn. If you are up to the challenge, go to it using this chapter as your starting point. But if you don't feel comfortable with building either of these, borrow some ideas from here and work with a professional landscaper on the design—to save some money, maybe you can lend a hand in building the feature (for more on hiring a landscape professional, see Chapter 12).

SHADE STRUCTURES

One of the greatest places to be on a sweltering summer day is under the roof of a sweeping porch overlooking the garden, nursing a tall iced tea. A friend of mine owns a turn-of-the-century bed-and-breakfast in western Massachusetts with just such a porch. Hers is so large that you can sit through one of summer's frequent thunder-storms and not feel a drop of rain, yet you can continue to enjoy the luxury of the cozy outdoor porch. Most of us aren't lucky enough to own an old home with a grand porch, so we have to find our shade elsewhere, whether it be under a shade structure like a gazebo or in a hammock under a pair of shade trees (see the photo above).

The object of garden shade, as I see it, is strictly human comfort in the midst of the landscape. The ideal retreat should provide a suitable amount of shade. It should also be located in the garden or near it and be large enough to suit your needs, depending on whether you want to share the space with others or on whether you want it to be a private getaway. It should also match the style of the yard and the home so that it does not look out of place.

A shade structure can be attached to a house (see the photo below), or it can be freestanding. The size and spacing of posts, joists, and beams, as well as the size of the concrete footings that the posts are anchored to, will depend on the size of the structure and on the load requirements. Typical sizes are 4x4 posts with 2x8 beams and joists. But it may be more in scale to use 6x6 posts and 2x10 beams and joists. You should consult

with your local building-code officials to determine the sizing of these parts and to find out any other local code requirements (for instance, whether or not a building permit is needed). This section will give you ideas on how to design a shade structure.

When choosing lumber, make sure all wood that will contact the ground is rot resistant. Use cedar,

An attached shade structure should fit into the landscape. This one serves as a transitional "room" between the house and garden, with shade provided by climbing vines.

greenheart, redwood, or pressure-treated lumber. Any wood that is not pressure treated should be stained or painted to protect it from the elements and should not contact the ground.

Attached structure

An attached shade structure can act as a transitional room connecting the house to the garden or a pool.

Although the framework for an attached structure is pretty simple, it is considered part of the house and must be anchored to the house via a 2x ledger, which is lag-bolted to the house framing (see the drawing below). The size of the ledger and the means of attachment will depend on the load require-

ATTACHED SHADE STRUCTURE

An attached shade structure is part of the house and needs solid support from the posts and from the ledger, which is tied into the house framing.

Metal hurricane tie

Beam

Joists

Metal joist hanger

Ledger

The post is anchored to a concrete footing sized according to the load requirements.

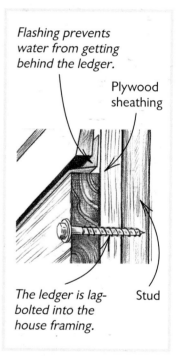

Flashing prevents water from getting behind the ledger.

Plywood sheathing

The ledger is lag-bolted into the house framing.

Stud

DEGREES OF SHADE

The size and spacing of the shade material will dictate the amount of shade provided. Aside from 2xs and vines, you can also provide shade by using canvas sheeting, lattice, bamboo, or woven reed.

LIGHT SHADE

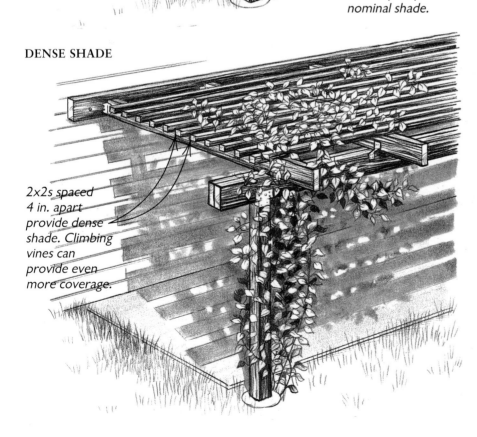

2x4s on edge spaced 12 in. apart provide nominal shade.

DENSE SHADE

2x2s spaced 4 in. apart provide dense shade. Climbing vines can provide even more coverage.

ments—again, check your local building code. It's also important to add flashing behind the ledger to prevent water from getting behind the siding and into the house walls.

To provide the shading, you can leave the joists exposed and space them closer together, planting climbing vines so that they will cover the structure, or you can place 2x4s or 2x2s on top of the joists. The closer the 2xs are spaced, the less sunlight that will get in, and vice versa (see the drawings at left). Alternate shade materials are lattice, woven reed or bamboo rolls, and canvas sheeting. (If you choose a solid shade material, such as canvas sheeting, the joists will need to be pitched to shed rainwater.)

FINISHED BEAM ENDS

To lessen the heavy, boxy look of beams and joists, sculpt their ends.

Bevel

Long bevel

Roundover

Scallop

Inverse or inverted roundover

To lessen the heavy, boxy look of the beams and joists, you can design sculpted ends on them. Bevel or round over the ends or make your own design (see the bottom right drawings on the facing page). If you're building the deck yourself, it's pretty easy to reproduce the design exactly on each member. Draw the pattern on a piece of cardboard or ¼-in. plywood and cut it out to use it as a template. Then simply place the template on each member and use a jigsaw to cut out the pattern.

Freestanding structure

A freestanding structure may be simple like an arbor or trellis (see the photo at right), or it can have a more complicated design with walls and floors like a gazebo (see the photo below). Whichever you

A simple freestanding structure like an arbor is easy to build.

A gazebo is an elegant hideaway but requires a lot of carpentry skills to build.

prefer, be sure to choose a size that will not overwhelm the garden and that will fit in with the house style and the yard.

An advantage to building a free-standing shade structure is that you can buy prefabricated buildings—trellises, arbors, and gazebos—at most home centers and some mail-order catalogs (see Sources on p. 162). These building kits come with complete instructions. You just bring home the building in pieces and assemble it on site.

If you are building a freestanding wood structure, the size and spacing of posts, beams, and rafters will be dictated by the load requirements. A gazebo will have to be designed to carry a heavier load than a trellis, for instance. As with an attached structure, check with local building officials to see if there are any special requirements. Some municipalities will require a building permit.

Shear forces are the biggest danger to a freestanding structure. Shear is lateral movement caused by wind and gravity. To prevent the structure from collapsing like a set of dominoes (called racking) or from swaying in the wind, shear braces must be added on the ends of the posts, as shown in the drawing below.

WATER GARDENS

Water gardens have become fixtures in American gardens, and there isn't a serious gardener who doesn't plan one for a serene spot somewhere in the yard. The most important design consideration is that the water garden look natural in its setting. You don't want it to look man-made, like a Hollywood set.

A large water garden may allow space to build a babbling brook (see the photo on p. 96) that melds naturally into the landscape. A smaller space limits the design possibilities. But even the smallest of water gardens can blend in well with the landscape as long as plants and rocks are placed so that they look natural (see the photo on the facing page).

A water garden requires a lot of planning and brawn. Your local landscape dealer might be able to give you some tips on how to construct it, and there are many articles and books that describe the process in detail (see Further Reading on p. 161). But it's not a project for the faint of heart. If you prefer, and if you can afford it, contract with a professional landscaper to do the job (for more on hiring a professional, see Chapter 12). To build the garden yourself, follow these basic installation steps.

Digging

The first step is digging the pool. With a small water garden, you'll get by with a shovel, but renting a skid-steer loader will make a larger excavation easier. Before digging, contact your local utilities to be sure that no buried water, gas, or electrical lines are in the way.

It's important to know what types of aquatic plants you want in the garden because some varieties grow better at a specific depth. An easy way to accommodate plants that thrive at different depths is to dig shelves into the pool that will allow

SHEAR BRACING

Simple 2x4 braces attached to the posts and beams prevent the structure from racking under shear forces.

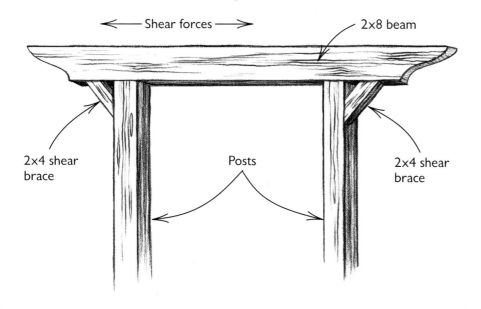

← Shear forces →

2x8 beam

2x4 shear brace

Posts

2x4 shear brace

A water garden doesn't have to be large. This small water garden fits comfortably into a niche in the landscape and supports water lilies.

WATER GARDEN

Rocks are placed naturally around the edges to hold the butyl liner in place. When combined with plantings, the rocks also help ease the transition from pool to earth.

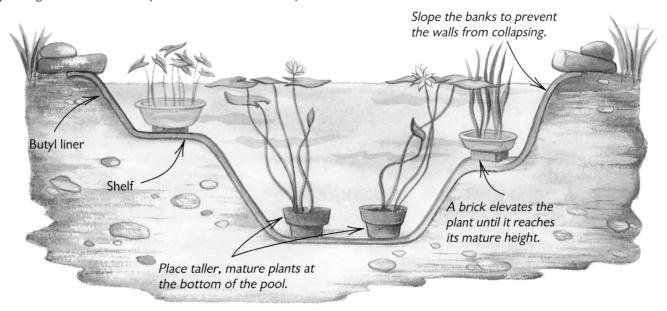

Slope the banks to prevent the walls from collapsing.

Butyl liner

Shelf

A brick elevates the plant until it reaches its mature height.

Place taller, mature plants at the bottom of the pool.

plants to thrive in both shallow and deeper water. In general, plan on making shelves 15 in. to 24 in. below the surface, although some lilies need a depth of 36 in.

Slope the banks of the pool away from the center to make a smooth transition from water to earth and to keep the edges from collapsing. Also be sure to compact the surfaces to minimize settling.

PLANTS FOR A WATER GARDEN

Here are a few plants that will brighten up any water garden (some are even beneficial to the water).

• Oxygenating plants like *Ranunculus Aquatilis* (water crowfoot) and *Elodea canadensis* (Canadian pondweed) will help keep the water clean.

• Floating plants like *Stratiotes aloides* (water soldier) will provide food and shade for fish and will deter algae growth.

• *Nymphaea sp.* (water lilies) like rich, fertile soil and should be planted in tubs on shelves under the water's surface. Two of my favorites are 'Leopardess' (photo 1) and 'Venus' (photo 2). Water lilies suitable for small pools include pink-flowering 'Mary Patricia', red 'James Brydon', yellow-blooming 'Helvola', and copper-orange 'Graziella'.

• Other plants that will survive in submerged tubs and that will add interesting color and shape to the garden include *Iris Kaempferi* (Japanese iris) (photo 3), *Typha minima* (dwarf cattail) (photo 4), and *Caltha palustris* (marsh marigold) (photo 5).

Installing the liner and pump

Once the excavation has been completed, add the liner. You can use a preformed rigid plastic pool, available from mail-order water-garden houses such as Lilypons or from garden centers, or you can use heavy-gauge butyl sheeting available at garden and home centers.

If a pump is to move water from one pool to another, install it after the

liner is in. The piping should be installed at this time too. Before going any further in the installation, test the pumping system. If it works, finish placing stones around the pool. The last group of stones hold the liner down, but they must also be placed as naturally as possible. The water garden should look like it's been around longer than your house.

Adding plants

The final step is adding the plants to the garden (for a list of plants suitable for a water garden, see pp. 104-105). It's a good idea to grow the aquatic plants in tubs placed on the shelves in the pool so that you can keep their rampant nature in check. The tubs will also allow you to lift out any plants that need overwintering in cold climates. For young, small plants, place the tubs on bricks and remove the bricks when the plants have matured.

Plant the edges of the pool with large- and long-leafed, drooping plants like hosta, ferns, and daylilies. These types of plants will hang over the rocks and will cover any rough edges, adding to the transition from earth to water.

Mix the long, leafy plants with spiky-leafed plants like grasses, iris, and liatris for a change in texture. As the landscape moves away from the pool, increase the size of the plants for a layered design that harmonizes the entire scheme.

If there are trees near the garden, place a screen over the pool in the fall to keep leaves out. Organic matter in the pool will foul the water with methane gas, which will in turn kill plants.

FINISHING TOUCHES

Adding ornamentation to your garden is the icing on the cake, the star on the Christmas tree. It allows you to add features that make the garden reflect your personality and style, making it an extension of you, whether it be sculpture or furniture.

I have a passion for frogs, so in my rock garden, I have scattered about whimsical sculptures of frogs: One sits reclining with his front legs folded behind his head, another naps in a corner, arms folded across his bloated belly (photo 1), and yet another—this one with an attitude—stands at the top of a slope, arms on his hips, surveying his property. I also have several other, more-conventional, amphibious rascals scattered around on other rocks. Your passion may be more toward pink flamingos and gazing balls, but any ornament, whimsical or otherwise, is worthy of a spot in the garden.

You can choose to be subtle or obvious when placing the ornamen-tation. One of the most amusing garden sculptures I know of (and one of my favorites) is located in the walled garden at the summer house at Fort Ticonderoga in New York. On one side of the garden, a gargoyle sits on a brick wall, tending a miniature cannon. Directly opposite, over 100 ft. away, is another gargoyle with a tiny cannonball in his mouth.

Where you locate the sculpture will dictate whether it will be subtle or the focal point, so careful placement is a must. Tuck little critters into the foliage to give a visitor a surprise, or slip a birdbath into the center of a garden, waiting to be found (photo 2). A great way to add a whimsical, subtle sculpture to the yard is to dress up a water spigot with a sculptured faucet (photo 3). It will bring a smile to the face of the person turning on the hose.

For a more dramatic effect, place sculpture (photo 4) or a large fountain in a prominent location. Put it at the end of a path, so the piece can be seen at the

beginning of the path, creating interest as a visitor walks toward it.

The furniture you choose is also a reflection of your personality, and it, like the sculptures, should be chosen and placed with care. Furniture can retreat to the background and harmonize with the venue, such as wrought iron in a formal garden on a brick patio (photo 5), or a rock bench among the ferns on a mulch path (photo 6). Or furniture can become the focal point of an area, as with brightly painted Adirondack chairs and boldly striped pillows on a wicker settee.

CHAPTER 9
Establishing a Lawn

There isn't a part of the yard and landscape that receives more attention than the lawn. As matter of fact, many homeowners are obsessed with it. I, for one, have a love/hate relationship with my lawn. I hate some of the maintenance required for upkeep, but I love walking barefoot on my lawn. And my recent passion—golf—has made me appreciate the care other people take to create and maintain a perfect lawn.

The most difficult part of integrating a lawn in your landscape plan is planting it. Establishing a lawn requires a lot of preparation and hard work, but if done correctly, you'll end up with a thriving lawn that just begs for bare feet. There are two methods used to establish a lawn: planting seed or laying sod. And regardless of which method you choose, the first step—preparing the base—is the same.

PREPARING THE BASE

Before planting seed or laying sod, you must prepare a base of topsoil that will support the lawn. First, the yard must be properly graded (for more on grading, see Chapter 3) and well compacted.

For a proper lawn base, you'll need at least 4 in. of topsoil. Test the existing soil to determine what nutrients are needed (for more on soil testing, see Chapter 2). And you should ask advice of a landscape contractor or soil specialist at your local testing lab about the texture and water-holding capacity of your soil to be sure it will support a lawn. If you must bring in new topsoil to augment the existing topsoil, make sure you have it tested before it is brought on site.

Once you have a 4-in. topsoil base in place, finish-grade it with a grading rake (see the photo at right), which has a wide head with teeth that catch small rocks and debris near the surface. The grading rake will make an absolutely smooth and graded surface to accept the seed or sod. How well you do the finish-grading will dictate how much cursing you will be doing later when the lawnmower scalps a high area or kicks out

A grading rake removes all the stones left near the surface of the topsoil by machines and makes an absolutely smooth surface to accept seed or sod.

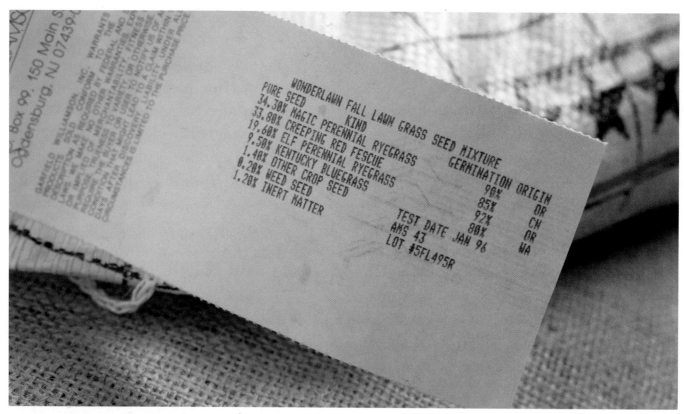

WONDERLAWN FALL LAWN GRASS SEED MIXTURE
PURE SEED   KIND   GERMINATION ORIGIN
34.30% MAGIC PERENNIAL RYEGRASS   96%   OR
33.80% CREEPING RED FESCUE   85%   OR
19.60% ELF PERENNIAL RYEGRASS   92%   CN
9.50% KENTUCKY BLUEGRASS   80%   OR
1.40% OTHER CROP SEED
0.20% WEED SEED
1.20% INERT MATTER   TEST DATE JAN 96
                                AMS 43   WA
                                LOT #5FL495R

Read the contents of the seed bag to find the percentages of different types of seed that are inside. What seeds are in the mix will determine the look of the lawn.

rocks as you mow. Once you are satisfied with the finish-grading, you can begin planting seed or laying sod.

PLANTING SEED

Although seeding will not give you instant results, it is an effective way of establishing a lawn. As a matter of fact, in some parts of the country, seeding gives as fine a result as laying sod. Plus it is less expensive.

Autumn is the best time to seed a lawn because the temperatures are lower, activating growth. Also, rainfall is more prevalent, and weeds are less apt to establish, especially annual weeds that will die with the frost. Unfortunately, it is usually necessary to reseed some spots in the spring where runoff occurred and carried the seeds away. If you must seed during

spring or summer, you'll need to water more frequently and heavily to germinate the seeds, and weeds may become a nuisance. There are three steps to planting seed: choosing the seed mix, spreading it, and watering and mowing.

Choosing a seed mix

When choosing a seed mix, keep future care in mind. What's in the bag will determine how the lawn will eventually look. So read the contents carefully to find the percentages of different seeds in the mix (see the photo above).

Although "conservation mix" sounds good, it is a marketing ploy. Usually, it has a large percentage of perennial clover and annual grasses. Clover is vigorous and competitive and will take over, choking out the good grasses. It also attracts bees, which may or may not be desirable to you. Clover does have one advantage in that it fixes nitrogen in the soil, making it possible to reduce the amount of fertilizer needed. As for the annual grasses in the mix, they will die with the first frost, leaving a lot of space for weeds to infiltrate the lawn during the next growing season.

A mix with a high percentage of Kentucky bluegrass, although it is a very desirable grass, will need constant fertilization to keep it healthy and competitive. Kentucky bluegrass is not as vigorous as other grasses and needs a lot of added nitrogen. The grass is also intolerant of shade.

The best balance, I think, mixes a low percentage of annual rye (say 10% to 15%) with perennial rye, creeping fescues, and tall fescues. The annual rye germinates in about three days, which guards against erosion and shades the ground while the other seeds germinate, usually in about three weeks.

Check with a local nursery or cooperative-extension agent for more information on the best grass types for your area.

Regardless of which mix you choose, heed the soil-test results indicating what nutrients you need to add to the soil to build a healthy lawn.

Spreading fertilizer and seed

Both the soil and the weather must be dry to work the soil and to fertilize and seed a lawn. The texture of the soil will be ruined if it is worked when wet, and the materials will clump in the spreader if they are damp or wet.

It's hard to miss spots with a cyclone spreader, which hurls fertilizer or seed a distance, allowing you to overlap the rows to ensure coverage.

Before beginning, look at your landscape plan and mark off areas within the yard where planting beds, walkways, or patios are planned so that you don't waste seed in those spaces.

For seeding and fertilizing, a push-behind cyclone spreader (see the photo above) is the best type to use because it hurls the materials a distance, creating overlap so you won't miss spots as you do with a

MAINTAINING A LAWN

Some people want a perfect lawn but don't have the time to spend on its maintenance, so they spend a good penny having the lawn professionally maintained. However, most people can't afford the luxury of hiring a pro, and many don't want to spend every waking moment taking care of the lawn, so they live with an imperfect lawn and keep maintenance to a minimum. It's all a matter of personal preference.

One of my neighbors has an obsession with his lawn. He spends most of the spring, the entire summer, and part of the fall out in his yard taking care of the grass.

The biggest chores involving the lawn include watering, mowing, fertilizing, and fighting weeds. Watering can be a daily chore if you live in a dry area or if the summer is particularly hot. If there are no drought restrictions in your area during hot months, water a few times per week in the early morning to prevent the lawn from burning. Most lawns require 1 in. of water a week.

Mowing will have to be done at least once a week. Don't mow any shorter than 2½ in. and leave it longer (about 3 in.) in the hotter, drier parts of the growing season. Tall grass will retain moisture for longer periods of time. Leave grass clippings on the lawn for mulch, which add nutrients to the soil and conserve moisture.

Fertilizing is a difficult part of maintaining any lawn. It has to be done at least twice a year, and more when needed. A lawn needs fertilizing if you notice that its color isn't right and if you see weeds cropping up.

The type of fertilizer and the frequency of feeding will depend on two factors: the soil type and the type of grass you have planted. A soil test should be performed annually to determine what nutrients the grass needs and whether liming is necessary.

If you want a perfect lawn, you'll be at war with dandelions and other weeds. The only way to win this war is to be unmerciful, which means using chemical weed killers available at garden centers. Although effective, the downside to these products is that they are toxic to people and pets.

I don't mind if my lawn is not perfect. So I do the minimum: I fertilize twice a year and mow when I have to. But I don't like to waste a lot of water on it—so I live with a burned lawn in August. And I don't like to use chemical weed killers—so I live with dandelions and a few other weeds.

drop spreader. Calibrate the spreader to distribute the recommended amounts of fertilizer or seed (the bags will tell you the amounts needed according to the spreader type). A cyclone spreader is easy to calibrate.

Spread the fertilizer first. Fill the spreader on the driveway or other nongrowing surface because, if you accidentally drop a clump of fertilizer (or lime) on the lawn, seed may not grow there. Fertilize in two different directions. For instance, fertilize along the width of the yard, then fertilize lengthwise to cover any gaps. Avoid shooting fertilizer into planting beds or onto the driveway. A good-quality spreader can be adjusted so that you can avoid covering areas you don't want to.

The seeding method is the same as the fertilizing method. First seed along the width of the yard, then move lengthwise. Avoid seeding areas where grass is not planned.

After spreading the fertilizer and seed, work them in with a grading rake. Then lightly mulch with seed-free (sterile) straw to conserve moisture while the seeds germinate.

Watering and mowing

After you are finished fertilizing and seeding, it's time to water the lawn area. Set up a sprinkler and move it around the yard every day. Once one area is moist, move the sprinkler to a dry area.

Water in the early morning. If you do it in the middle of the day, the water will evaporate quickly and will not penetrate very well. The

Sod is rolled up and loaded onto pallets for shipping. If possible, store the sod in the shade and sprinkle it with water to keep it from drying out.

top inch of the soil must be kept moist at all times for the grass seed to germinate.

Once the lawn has been established, you can water less frequently because the grass will retain moisture. But you'll have to water for a longer time to allow it to penetrate deep enough to get to the grass roots. The deeper the water goes, the longer and stronger the grass roots will eventually be.

Mow as soon as the grass needs it. Don't worry about injuring the new grass. If you don't mow right away, the grass will lie down and be harder to mow. Mowing causes the grass plants to branch, creating a thicker, denser mass (for more on mowing and lawn maintenance, see the sidebar on the facing page).

LAYING SOD

Although expensive, there is nothing like the instant results of sod. However, even though the yard looks done once the sod has been installed, sodded areas must be mollycoddled until the grass roots establish. No foot traffic should be allowed, and the sod needs constant moisture to make the roots penetrate, or "take" to, the topsoil.

A smooth, continuous surface is critical for sod. Any dips may cause the sod to lose contact with the soil, allowing the roots to dry out, which means death for the grass.

Sod storage

Sod is delivered on pallets in strips rolled in 4-ft. to 6-ft. lengths (see the photo above). When it is on

Knit the sod joints together. Allow a little slack and lay them flat and as close together as possible without overlapping.

Because the rolls have straight edges, it's easier to start near a straight edge of the yard, such as a driveway or pool deck. If you don't have a straight reference, draw a straight line on the ground with a little lime and place the first roll there.

Place the next piece immediately adjacent to the previous. Alternate joint lines and keep them tight so that they remain imperceptible to the eye. Place the pieces as close as possible without overlapping, and knit the new piece into the previous pieces (see the photo at left). Pound the sod down with your fist to make sure it is completely contacting the soil everywhere.

Where the sod will meet a curved edge, such as the edge of a planting bed, overlap the sod into the bed. Then use a garden hose to lay out the curve and cut the sod with a shovel (see the top photo on the facing page) or a sod knife along the curve. You can buy a sod knife at hardware stores and garden centers.

Sod will start to dry out from the edges inward. Using a rake, spread topsoil to cover any exposed edges, such as those around a planting bed (see the bottom photo on the facing page). And place ½ in. or so of topsoil between the sod edges and any hard object, such as a concrete curb or driveway.

After laying the sod and filling the edges with topsoil, use a drum roller to ensure that the sod strips are contacting the ground. (You can rent a drum roller at an equipment

site, taking care of the rolls on the pallets is critical to their survival.

Try not to order more than what you will be laying in a day. But if you must, because the sod farm is far away or it won't deliver small amounts, try to store the sod in the shade. Sprinkle the rolls with water frequently to keep them from drying out, but don't overwater because the rolls will become a muddy mess and will be impossible to work with.

Sod placement

As with planting seed, autumn is a good time to lay sod. Don't wait too long into the season because it may become difficult to unroll the strips and lay the sod because of the lower temperatures.

Use a garden hose to guide you when cutting sod on a curve.

Use a rake to cover any exposed edges of the sod with soil to prevent the sod from drying out quickly.

DON'T BOTHER WITH GRASS IN THE SHADE

If you've ever tried to grow grass in the shade, you know it is an uphill battle. Even if you use grass-seed mixes specifically designated for the shade, it is a difficult proposition. Usually this is because the soil found in shade has a nutrient content unlike soil found in sunny conditions.

A shady yard is generally full of trees that play havoc with the pH and nutrient availability of the soil. Try as you might to alter the conditions, the soil will always be too acidic from leaf drop or evergreen-needle drop. The best crop you grow will be moss, which always wins when grass is its competition.

On the other hand, because of the leaves and needles dropping, the soil will be humus-rich from the resulting compost. This is a perfect environment for shade-loving ground covers, such as lily of the valley, lamium, and pachysandra, and for ferns. So give in to the lack of light and give up on the lawn in shaded areas.

Rolling sod with a drum roller ensures good contact with the soil beneath.

rental center). Fill the drum with water and roll the entire sodded area (see the photo above).

After rolling, water frequently (every morning) and deeply, and be sure no one walks on the lawn until the roots have established.

The amount of time needed for the roots to take varies, depending on the moisture and temperature. But once it happens, the sod will grow taller, indicating the lawn is ready for playing and for mowing.

CHAPTER 10

Planting Beds

Planting beds provide focal points in the landscape plan and dress up all the other features in the yard. If you were to imagine the landscape as a birthday cake, the planting beds would be the flowers. They add ornamentation, drawing attention to themselves, and yet tie the whole picture together. They can also be used to cover blemishes in the landscape, such as the house foundation or an animal pen.

PLANTS THAT ADD WINTER INTEREST

FOCAL POINTS

• For an interesting, upright focal point in a large planting bed, *Prunus Maackii* (Manchurian cherry) is a good choice. Its shiny, rich, red-brown mahogany bark peels just like a birch tree, and against the white of snow, it glistens (photo 1). It is extremely hardy (Zone 2), blooms white flowers and small black fruit, and adds yellow color to the yard in the fall.

• More common *Cornus alba* 'Sibirica' (red-twig dogwood) (photo 2) and *Cornus stolonifera* 'Flaviramea' (yellow-twig dogwood) are large, vigorous shrubs. They are perfect choices for an island planting bed in the yard or for a hedgerow. With chalk-white stems and yellow, edible berries, *Rubus biflorus* can add a ghostly touch to a red-brick wall.

GRASSES

• Any planting bed would benefit by the addition of ornamental grasses for their striking autumn wheat color and wispy, feathery dried flowers that hang on through winter. *Miscanthus* flowers look like miniature brooms, and *Cortaderia Selloana* (pampas grass) moves like graceful plumes in the breeze (photo 3). *Pennisetum* is bottle-brush-shaped, and *Festuca* flowers are loose and spikey. You'll find many sizes and cultivars for grasses, but choose appropriately for your hardiness zone.

EVERGREENS

• The usually bronze-green leaves of PJM rhododendrons turn reddish purple in the fall and hold their color through the winter. Many junipers become a lovely plum-purple color when cold weather sets in. Low, spreading types are appropriate for the front layer of a planting bed.

• Yellow-foliaged evergreens like *Chamaecyparis pisifera* 'Filifera Aurea' (photo 4) are striking focal points in the winter garden, still layered with that fan-shaped foliage.

WEEPING TREES

• One of my passions is weeping trees, and there are no better architectural plants for winter appeal. *Betula pendula* 'Youngii' (Young's weeping birch) has white, peeling bark, dark-brown stems, and twigs that cascade in streams from the mushroom-shaped head to the ground (photo 5).

• Some of my other favorite deciduous weeping trees include *Ulmus glabra* 'Camperdownii' (camperdown elm), *Caragana arborescens* 'Pendula' (weeping Siberian pea), and *Fagus sylvatica* 'Purpurea Pendula' (weeping purple beech).

• For corkscrew-branched sculptural specimens, there are none better than *Corylus Avellana* 'Contorta' (Harry Lauder's walking stick) (photo 6) and *Salix × erythroflexuosa* (corkscrew willow) with orange-yellow, pendulous, twisted, and contorted stems. Harry Lauder's can be kept under control as an addition to a foundation planting bed, but the willow is best planted out in the yard.

FRUIT

• The classic winter garden show features fruit in many colors: red, orange, yellow, blue, black, and white. The attraction draws furry and feathered guests, as well as our eyes, to feast. *Pyracantha coccinea* (fire thorn) is abundant with red (*P. coccinea* 'Watereri'), yellow (*P. coccinea* 'Shawnee'), or bright orange berries (*P. coccinea* 'Mohave') and can be grown as a shrub or pruned and trained into an espalier or bonsai specimen.

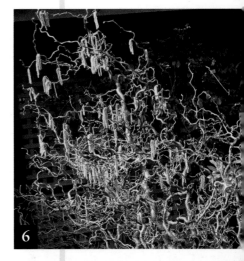

• For huge clusters of red fruit, *Ilex verticillata* 'Sparkleberry' (winterberry) is unmatched (photo 7), but it needs a pollinator to produce (try *I.* 'Apollo') and space to grow. It is best planted along the edge of the yard or in a woodland garden.

• Tiny, abundant, persistent, hanging crab apples are a key feature in a winter garden (photo 8). My favorite is *Malus Sargentii* (Sargent crab), which has a very horizontal branching habit and remains dwarf, providing a very architectural element as well. As long as enough space is left for Sargent crab to spread its 8-ft. to 10-ft. branches horizontally, its height, at 6 ft., will not intrude but will be a highlight in a foundation planting bed. Use low-growing perennials and ground covers to fill the space beneath its branches.

• *Viburnum trilobum* 'Alfredo' lives up to its common name, cranberry bush, by sporting large, shiny, clusters of edible, bright-red berries, perfect for jams and jellies. It stays 4 ft. tall and has brilliant red fall color as well.

All the planting beds should be drawn out on the landscape plan so that you know what plants will be going where (for more on drawing a landscape plan, see Chapter 4). Without a clear plan in mind and on paper, the yard will appear fragmented and unprofessional. But don't think of this as work. It's time to be creative and to have some fun.

DESIGNING PLANTING BEDS

The goal of any planting bed—whether it's an island bed in the middle of the yard or a foundation bed—should be to draw the eye to the big picture and then to create a pleasing composition of colors, textures, shapes, and sizes.

What ultimately makes the composition successful—and sets an extraordinary bed apart from an ordinary one—is the arrangement of the bed and the plants within it. For instance, a straight bed against the foundation, with plants in a straight line, is ordinary. But to turn the bed into a unique work of art, widen it, give it a curve, and layer the plants using contrast and repetition of colors, textures, shapes, and sizes.

Mixing color, texture, shape, and size adds depth and variety to a planting bed, while repetition ties all the elements within the bed together, drawing the eye from one side to the other.

Yearlong bloom and interest

Another thing to strive for in a planting bed is a succession of bloom during each of the seasons so that the garden is interesting during spring, summer, and fall.

Winter interest adds another dimension to a planting bed and becomes an important design component. Instead of laying the bed to rest for winter, plant varieties that have interesting shapes or colors during the cold months.

Shrubs and trees that look as engaging in the winter as they do during the growing season are the real gems of any garden. Some plants produce berries that persist into the winter; some have dried

An overgrown foundation planting bed crowds the landscape and obscures house views.

SHADE GARDENING

Look at gardening in the shade as an opportunity rather than a liability. As long as you use plants that are adapted to shady conditions, you will be successful.

Physiologically, the leaves of shade-loving plants are formed to accept only low light and in sun are likely to burn. Conversely, sun-loving plants will grow lanky and reach for light if planted in the shade.

So take care in choosing the right plants for the habitat you have. Follow the sun patterns in your yard, and if any bed receives a half a day or more of shade, it is a candidate for shade-loving plants. Should the shade be cast by trees that will lose leaves in the winter, it is wise to avoid evergreens like yews, rhododendrons, and hemlocks that will burn in winter sun and wind. Here's a list of plants that like the shade.

• *Pieris* (Andromeda azaleas) and *Leucothoe* (photo 1) are broad-leaved evergreens.

• Most viburnums and *Clethra* (photo 2) (try 'Hummingbird' at 2 ft. to 3 ft. in height) are deciduous shade lovers.

• Ferns and perennials like hosta, lily of the valley, *Astilbe* (photo 3), *Pulmonaria* (photo 4), *Lamium* (photo 5), and bleeding hearts will add foliage accents and color.

• Annuals like *Coleus* (photo 6), impatiens, and begonias will luminate a shady spot in the garden. I especially like white flowers and white-variegated foliage in a shade garden because they look electric in the low light (see the photo on p. 117).

flowers and seed pods; some have unusual bark or stem color; some evergreen leaves turn a different color; and other plants are sculpturally attractive without their leaves (for a list of plants that will add winter interest to your beds, see pp. 118-119).

An easy way to plan for season-long bloom in your planting beds is to put your plant choices into a chart—before you put them into the plan—and indicate the bloom or fruiting season and the color.

It's also important to pay attention to growth rates so that individual plants within each bed will mature at the rate you want them to. It's a good idea to indicate in the chart the mature height and spread of each plant you choose. The chart will help you draw the plants to size on the plan, and you'll quickly see where there will be gaps. You can fix gaps by rearranging the bed altogether or by filling them with annuals or ground covers.

Plant choices

Be sure the plants you include in your beds are appropriate for the exposure—whether it be sun or shade (for more shade gardening, see the sidebar on p. 121)—and for the hardiness zone in which you live (also consider micro-climates). And be sure that all of your plant choices are available at local garden centers or through a catalog. A list of plants that work well in an island planting bed is shown on the facing page. A list of plants that work well in a foundation planting bed is shown on pp. 130-131.

PLANTING BEDS NEAR THE FOUNDATION

One of the most difficult designs to achieve successfully is that of a foundation planting bed. All the rules for a typical planting bed apply, but there are other factors that come into play, such as the color of the house, the space available, and whether the goal of the bed is to hide an exposed foundation or to highlight a front entry (or both).

There are many schools of thought on how a foundation planting bed should look. Some gardeners prefer nothing but evergreens to "cozy up" the foundation, creating a row of trimmed, pointy plants.

There are those gardeners who prefer to create what I call green monsters, hiding the house with huge plants that become so overgrown that you can barely find the front door (see the photo on p. 120).

Then there's the minimalist school. In old England and early America, many folks created a "door yard," usually with utilitarian-type herb kitchen gardens (see the photo below). The spare design can be

The spareness of this door-yard planting bed is very appealing. It highlights but does not overwhelm the classic door and old masonry.

PLANTS FOR ISLAND BEDS

• For unmatched early spring elegance, shrubby *Magnolia stellata* (star magnolia) will knock your socks off (photo 1). Like its cousin saucer magnolia, star magnolia blooms before the leaves unfurl but with many-petaled, star-shaped, white blossoms. Star magnolia will become 6 ft. to 10 ft. tall and spread as wide, making it a perfect candidate for a focal point in the backyard.

• Trees not only work well in island beds, but they also may be used to establish shade on a patio or deck. Remember to leave enough space for spreading roots and branches. Near a pool or patio, where leaf drop is a problem in the fall,

trees in the oak family are an asset because they hang on to their leaves well into the winter. By then, the pool will be covered and the patio abandoned until spring. Crab apples and flowering dogwoods are classic trees (be sure to choose hybrids with disease and insect resistance). Unlike *Cornus florida* (flowering dogwood), *Cornus Kousa* (Chinese dogwood) blooms after the leaves come out a little later in the season. It is usually grown as a large shrub (photo 2).

• To create a focal point in the island bed, plant *Viburnum plicatum tomentosum* 'Shasta', (shasta doublefile viburnum) (photo 3). It has an extraordinary, late-spring flowering habit, and large white flowers line the completely horizontal branches, creating a texture contrast as well as eye-catching beauty. This is one of my signature plants—I always try to sneak it in somewhere, even in light shade. It will grow to 7 ft. or 8 ft. tall and will spread as wide.

• Midsize evergreens like *Juniperus* (seagreen juniper) and some spreading perennials like *Hemerocallis* (daylilies) are perfect for filling gaps in an island planting bed. I like all daylilies, even the orange escapes you see along the side of the road. For a cultivated, sunny border, say, around a light post, I mix early, mid, and late bloomers and colors for a continuous show throughout the season. The yellows usually bloom first, followed by pinks, reds, melons, lavenders, and bicolors. Daylilies, at 2½ ft. to 3½ ft. tall, soften corners as their foliage wraps the edges, even when they're not in bloom. The dwarf 'Stella D'Oro' (photo 4) is particularly outstanding, with a golden yellow that blooms for an extended period of time.

BACK LAYER OF A FOUNDATION PLANTING BED

When making a foundation planting bed, start with the back layer. Pull one or two of the plants forward to avoid planting in a straight line. Mix evergreen and deciduous plants for texture change, and use plants with year-round interest.

very effective. I know many people who still create door yards, but they typically live in old houses, with attractive masonry or stone walls to show off.

My school of thought, however, says to tie the foundation planting beds into the entire landscape by mixing and repeating colors, textures, shapes, and sizes. A straight design of the same plants is boring; overgrown trees and

shrubs that cover the entire house and block views and entries are crowded and unattractive; and planting beds that are too small could get lost against a house.

Layered plants

The most effective way to mix and repeat color, texture, shape, and size is to layer the plants in the bed.

For example, at the back of the bed, near the foundation, place taller plants so that they undulate

MIDDLE LAYER OF A FOUNDATION PLANTING BED

The middle layer has plants of intermediate size but could include a focal-point tree or large shrub. The focal-point plant should be pulled forward of the others to draw attention to it and to allow it to grow large. Some plants in this middle layer may die back in the winter.

along the foundation wall (see the drawing on the facing page). Here you can mix evergreens and deciduous plants to create an interesting texture of green needles, flowers, and leaves.

The middle layer can include a vertical focal point like a narrow weeping tree (see the drawing above). Low shrubs fill the gaps between the larger ones, weaving back and forth in the rear. Taller perennials and grasses will also work for the middle of the bed.

The front layer of the bed can have an edging of perennials like hostas, low shrubs like spindle tree (*Euonymus fortunei* 'Emerald Gaiety'), and ground covers like ivy (*Hedera*), bugleweed (*Ajuga*), stonecrop, orpine (*Sedum*), and spurge (*Pachysandra*). Covering as

FRONT LAYER OF A FOUNDATION PLANTING BED

The front layer of a foundation planting bed usually consists of perennials and bulbs as well as low-growing shrubs.

Ground-cover plants such as *Ajuga* 'Burgundy Glow' reduce weeds and conserve moisture while providing an attractive front layer in any garden.

much of the bed as possible with plants reduces weeds and conserves moisture, but try not to overcrowd it (see the drawing on the facing page).

If you are planting beds on two sides of an entry, it is not necessary to create identical beds on both sides. Instead, use the same plants or different plants of the same colors and arrange them differently on both sides. Just keep it balanced. For instance, use one large, red-flowering plant on one side of the front door and three smaller red-flowering plants on the other side to achieve both balance and repetition (see the drawing on p. 128).

ACHIEVING BALANCE AND REPETITION

Repeating the color of flowers or foliage draws the eye across the planting bed. Here, a large shrub on one side of the door is balanced on the other side with three smaller ones of the same color. Notice the contrast in leaf texture but the similarities in leaf color, in flower shape, and in flower color.

PLANTING THE BEDS

Once you have your design on paper and your plants in hand, you can finally head out to the garden and get down and dirty. Although it's hard work, this is the fun part for most gardeners.

Dig

The first step in planting is digging, but don't dig the hole deeper than where the soil line ends on the balled-and-burlapped plant or container. A plant set too deep will suffocate from too much soil on its roots.

Before digging, hold the shovel next to the plant and make a mark at the point on the shovel's handle that is level with the top of the root ball (see the drawing below). Then you can use the mark as a guide to dig to the correct depth. Make a real effort not to dig the

DIGGING TO THE CORRECT DEPTH

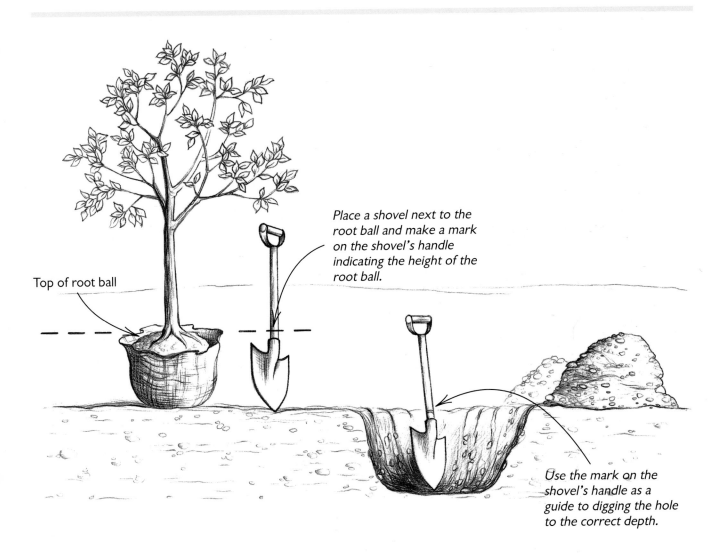

Top of root ball

Place a shovel next to the root ball and make a mark on the shovel's handle indicating the height of the root ball.

Use the mark on the shovel's handle as a guide to digging the hole to the correct depth.

FOUNDATION PLANTS

• The most common evergreen foundation plant is *Taxus* (yew). It has been so overused that hybridizers have developed virtually any shape and size yew imaginable. In reality, yews only do well in a partially shaded situation, and in colder climates, on the protected north or east side of the house. They are often pruned into shapes, some ghastly and unnatural, which often causes the lower limbs to die out from lack of light. With age and neglect, they become leggy and overgrown. I suggest choosing a slow-growing dwarf variety like *Taxus cuspidata* 'Nana'.

• *Abies balsamea* 'Nana' (dwarf balsam fir) has rich, green color, grows slowly, and stays compact.

• For an upright evergreen, try *Chamaecyparis obtusa* 'Nana Gracilis' (dwarf Hinoki cypress). It is bright green with fan-shaped sprays of foliage (photo 1).

• One of my favorite blue-gray-leaved evergreens is *Picea Omorika* 'Nana' (dwarf Serbian spruce), which keeps a rounded and compact habit (photo 2).

• *Picea Abies* 'Nidiformis' (bird's-nest spruce) is a very slow-growing ground-cover evergreen. I like to use it in groups of three around a lamp post or at the beginning of a walkway as a reliable greeting plant, foiling bright perennials like 'Stella D'Oro' daylilies.

• Broad-leaved evergreens are the bonus plants of the garden. Their leaves resemble, in many cases, deciduous plants, but they don't drop off when the weather gets cold. It is very easy, though, to choose plants like large-leaved *rhododendrons* that get big and out of scale in the foundation planting bed. Small-leaved culti-vars like PJM, 'Olga Mezitt', and Wilson are far more easy to main-tain in the foundation planting bed. PJM has bright-pink flowers in the spring, remains compact and up-right, even into age, and is very hardy to Zone 4.

• *Kalmia* (mountain laurel) and *Buxus* (boxwoods) can become large and need pruning. But a plant like *Mahonia Aquifolium* (Oregon grape holly) stays 3 ft. to 6 ft. tall and looks like a holly (photo 3).

• *Syringa* 'Miss Kim lilac' stays 3 ft. to 4 ft. tall and has a very rounded habit. It blooms profusely a little later in the spring than its larger counterparts.

• *Spiraea nipponica* 'Snowmound' (photo 4) bears the beautiful white flowers of the old-fashioned bridal wreath, but stays smaller, denser, and less arching. Other spiraeas like 'Anthony Waterer' (photo 5) and 'Little Princess' make perfect middle-layer plants and produce flat, pink flowers in early summer.

• *Weigela* 'Rhumba' grows to about 4 ft. and 'Minuet' to about 2 ft.—ideal flowering plants for midseason. Their long, bell-shaped dark-pink flowers are very attractive to hummingbirds.

• *Daphne* 'Carol Mackie' (photo 6) produces lovely, white-edged variegated green foliage, light-pink flowers in early spring, and a

sweet lingering scent. It is an outstanding accent plant to place near the edge of the bed so the fragrance will be appreciated. It lasts about seven years, and you'll enjoy every minute of it and replace it with the same thing—believe me.

• One of the few plants spectacular for late-season bloom is *Hydrangea*, and 'PeeGee' fits the scale of a foundation planting bed quite well (photo 7). The huge snowball-like flowers appear in late summer, become tawny pink as the temperatures get colder, and finally turn brown with the frost, hanging on for winter interest. They are perfect for dried-flower bouquets.

• *Caryopteris* 'Blue Mist' (photo 8) grows 3 ft. to 5 ft. tall and has profuse, tiny, bright royal-blue flowers in late summer and aromatic, soft silvery green leaves. I have a 3-ft.-tall plant that dies back about 12 in. each year. But a judicious pruning of the dead wood first thing in the spring produces a lush flush of growth and flowers that bees and hummingbirds won't leave alone.

hole too deep. But if you do, add soil to the bottom of the hole. Make sure you compact the soil to remove air pockets that will dry out the roots and ultimately kill the plant. Actually stomp around in the hole, even if it's only with one foot, trying to level the soil as you compact it.

Once the hole is at the proper depth, widen it enough so that the plant will not be shoehorned into the hole. Dig about 6 in. to 1 ft. wider than the plant's root ball all the way around.

Plant

Remove all packaging, such as burlap, plastic containers, or wire baskets, from the roots of the plant. Place the plant in the center of the hole, turn it to expose its best side for viewing, and backfill. After backfilling, make sure you compact the soil around the plant. Use the heel of your shoe to remove air pockets, and, as I mentioned before, don't be afraid to stomp!

I do not recommend changing or amending the soil before backfilling except to add organic matter or peat moss when necessary. These amendments should be well mixed into the backfill. Don't just dump them in. If you make the soil in the hole so much richer in nutrients than the surrounding soil, there is no incentive for the roots to grow beyond the hole. The roots just wind around and girdle themselves in an effort to avoid the less-desirable soil beyond the hole. This will not allow the roots to grow

enough to anchor the plant, which will make it unstable, and it will eventually kill the plant.

When the hole has been filled, make a saucer or dam with soil around the base of the plant to capture water.

Stake trees

If you've planted trees in the bed, the next step is staking. Any tree, evergreen or deciduous, taller than 8 ft. should be staked.

I've grown trees in Vermont for several years now. When we dig one out of the nursery, it has been growing there for at least four years. During that time, the tree has spread its roots well beyond the size of its crown, or head. The roots not only take in nutrients, but they also anchor the tree to the ground. When it is dug up, the longer anchoring roots are chopped off, leaving a root ball only about 30 in. across. Because the tree lacks those anchoring roots, it is necessary to provide supplemental support when it is planted.

When staking a tree, the stakes and wires must be taut to be effective; otherwise, the staking is just window dressing. So follow these important steps to best anchor your trees until they can support themselves, which will usually take at least one full growing season. The steps are different for deciduous trees and for evergreen trees. You can use either hardwood or softwood stakes, but unless

the hardwood stakes are pressure treated, hemlock or pine will last longer.

For a deciduous tree, cut two 2x2 stakes at least 6 ft. long. Put a point on one end to make it easier to drive into the ground.

Next, decide from where the prevailing winds blow and insert the stakes about 2 ft. from the stem, exactly opposite each other, on the side of the wind (see the left drawing on the facing page). If wind is not a factor, place the stakes where they will be the least obtrusive to your view.

Drive the stakes vertically at least 2 ft. into the ground. Keeping the stake vertical will help hold the wire taut. If you hit a rock, lift out the stake and move it slightly to keep it upright. For aesthetics, try to bury the stakes so they are the same height above ground. If you need to, saw off a few inches at the top to make them equal.

After the stakes have been driven into the ground, cut two 18-in. pieces of an old garden hose and then cut two 5-ft.-long pieces of flexible electric-fence wire. You can get this type of wire at most hardware stores.

Slip the hose sections over each length of wire and slide them to the middle. Then straddle the wire around the tree just below the 4-ft. mark. The hose sections will protect the trunk of the tree from being cut by the wire. Pull both ends of the wire toward a stake, parallel to the ground.

Twist the wire ends together on the outside of the stake and snip off any excess. Repeat the steps for the other length of wire on the other stake. After both wires have been attached to the stakes, use the handle of your pruners (inserted between the stake and tree) to twist the wires taut. Slide the pruners between the wires and rotate until all the slack has been removed. Repeat on the other side. You can also use long eye bolts or U-bolts to secure the wire, which allows tightening as needed.

For an evergreen tree, cut three 2x2 stakes about 4 ft. long and put a point on their ends. Three stakes are needed here because an evergreen has a bigger spread of branches and tends to need more support (see the right drawing below). Drive the stakes at least 2 ft. into the ground at a 45° angle, about 2 ft. from the tips of the

STAKING TREES

DECIDUOUS

Cut 6-ft. stakes and bury them 2 ft. below the ground. Keep them as vertical as possible.

EVERGREEN

Cut 4-ft. stakes and bury them at a 45° angle 2 ft. below the ground.

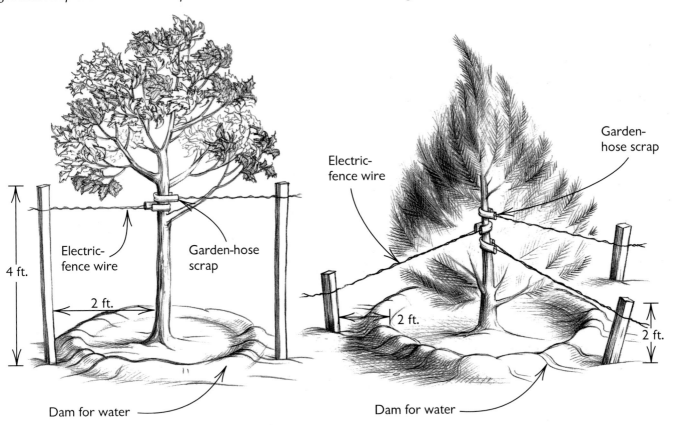

Electric-fence wire

Garden-hose scrap

4 ft.

2 ft.

Dam for water

Garden-hose scrap

Electric-fence wire

2 ft.

2 ft.

Dam for water

lower branches. Space the stakes evenly around the tree to provide equal support on all sides.

Wrap the wires around the stem at the 4-ft. mark and attach them the same way as with a deciduous tree, twisting the wires taut.

Mulch

After putting all the plants in place, spread about 2 in. to 3 in. of shredded bark mulch around all the plants and in between to fill the beds. But don't fill too deeply with it because a deep layer of mulch can smother the plants. The mulch will break down over time, revealing bare patches of earth, and should be replenished every few years.

Mulch serves several purposes. It conserves moisture, cools the soil in summer, and insulates the ground in winter. Although mulch will not prevent weeds altogether because wind and wildlife will drop them on the planting bed, it will limit their growth (plus weeds are infinitely easier to pull out of mulch than out of soil). I do not put a layer of weed cloth under the mulch because weed cloth makes it diffi-cult to move plants around or to divide perennials. It is also rendered useless as soon as a shovel is put in the bed, slicing the cloth, and mulch always seems to slide off, leaving the cloth exposed.

Water

After spreading the mulch, it's time to water the plants. The key to watering—both young and old plants—is providing even moisture. By even, I mean consistent: don't let the plants dry out and don't waterlog them.

New plants require a good soaking when they are planted to get the water down to the roots. A soaking means standing with a hose for at least 15 minutes. They should be watered about four times per week.

Once a plant has established its roots, which usually takes a full growing season, continue watering. Don't rely on the rain to do this job adequately. It will not take the place of a hosing. The best time of day to water is early in the morning, before the heat of the day sets in. Water evaporates quickly in the middle of the day, and watering at night encourages fungi growth. (If leaves are droopy in the evening, however, I make an exception to watering at night.)

There are two dangers associated with watering: underwatering, which dries out roots and kills plants, and overwatering, which creates a swampy, waterlogged area. Many fungal diseases thrive in this environment.

How much watering you have to do after the plant has established roots depends on the type of plant you have (perennials need less water than trees) and on the type of soil you have and whether it has good water-holding capacity (for more on soil, see Chapter 2).

The best test to see if the plant needs water is to stick your fingers down into the soil around the plants. If you only feel moisture on the surface or the top inch of the soil, there is no water at the roots. That means you should step up your watering schedule.

Finally, don't stop watering when the weather gets cool; water right up until the ground freezes. That way, when there is a temporary thaw in January or February, there will be a ready supply of water for the roots. That thaw period is actually when many plants winter-kill because they get the signal to grow from the increase in temperature and light, and they grope around for water. Finding none, they dry out and are unable to withstand the fluctuating temperatures of the late winter, early spring, and the early call to come out of dormancy.

CHAPTER 11
Specialty Gardens

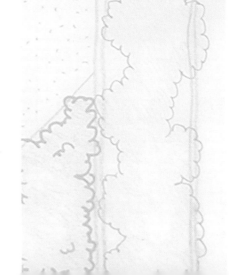

Specialty gardens offer opportunities to create pockets of interest within the landscape, sprinkling it with color and even with scents. Specialty gardens allow gardeners to put their final stamp on the landscape. And they are not just for large yards. Any-size yard can benefit from the addition of a specialty garden.

Placing taller plants in the middle of a perennial island garden allows you to see all the plants as you walk around it.

Some of the most interesting and fun specialty gardens to build are perennial gardens, herb gardens, container gardens, rock gardens, and edible gardens. The plants you include in these gardens and how you arrange them are only limited by your imagination. What I offer here are some ideas to get you started.

PERENNIAL GARDENS

Some novice gardeners are intimidated by the thought of stepping beyond the comfort of planting near the foundation. But planting a perennial garden is not as difficult as it may seem, and it's a great way to experiment with

colors and sizes and different combinations thereof.

What should make a perennial garden even more appealing to a novice is that if you don't like the combinations you chose or if the sizing didn't work out quite right, it's easy to move perennials around. Don't be afraid to make mistakes. It's really the only way to learn about plants and their habits. To make a perennial garden, you can mix colors and sizes or use the same plants and colors. It's pretty simple.

Start with a small plot of earth, about 10 ft. by 4 ft. Soften the edges by adding curves at the corners or by making the front edge

flow in a serpentine fashion. Remove all the sod from the garden area, incorporate some well-rotted compost or manure, and you're ready to plant.

Lay out all the plants before digging so you can space them properly and make a last check of the design. If there's some sort of backdrop to the garden, such as a fence or a stone wall, layer the perennials, with taller plants to the rear. If you can walk around the garden, taller plants should be in the middle, graduating in size to the edges all the way around (see the photo above). As with other gardens I've discussed, mix and repeat color, size, shape, and texture to draw the eye across the whole garden and to specific areas within it.

Research the plants you want to put in to make sure you know their mature sizes, their colors, and their bloom times. An easy way to check and compare this information is to make a chart of all the plants (for more on designing planting beds, see Chapter 10). I try to locate plants with long blooming times where they will fill gaps between other short-season bloomers (for a list of perennials, see pp. 138-139).

When planting, dig each hole separately, put the plant in the hole, backfill, and then compact the soil around the plant with your feet to remove any air pockets (for more on planting, see pp. 129 and 132-134).

Many clients of mine request perennial gardens that use only one or two colors, such as an all-white flowering garden or a garden with only shades of blue. Other popular themes include gardens with only evening- and night-blooming flowers—called a moon garden—gardens with plants that have variegated leaves, and gardens that use only scented flowers. If you want a fragrant garden, be sure to locate it so that passersby will be able to appreciate the scents (for a list of fragrant plants, see pp. 146-147).

CONTAINER GARDENS

For those with limited time or space, or for people with physical limitations, who still would like the enjoyment of gardening, the best option is to plant in containers

Containers house vegetables as well as flowers in a sunny spot on this deck.

PERENNIALS

SUN LOVERS

• *Coreopsis* 'Moonbeam' is a perpetually blooming basket of sunshine (photo 1). It is covered with small yellow flowers starting in early summer and continuously blooming through the fall.

• A perennial with a different growth habit is *Liatris* 'Kobold' (photo 2). This summer-blooming perennial has dark-pink spiky flowers to contrast the flat daisy-like ones of *Coreopsis*. It reaches 18 in. to 24 in. tall, adding vertical interest to the perennial garden, and loves full sun.

• *Campanula persicifolia* 'Alba' is upright (photo 3), with stems about 2 ft. to 3 ft. tall and large, bell-shaped white flowers, 1 in. to 1½ in. across. The blue varieties are just as lovely.

• For early spring bloom, *Anemone Pulsatilla* (the Pasque flower), which grows 8 in. to 12 in. tall, combines gray-white fluffy hairs on its stem with bell-shaped, 2-in. blooms of purple, white, or red (photo 4). The fluff remains long after the flowers go by, adding another texture to the garden.

• Most people are familiar with the old-fashioned bearded irises, but my choice is *Iris sibirica* (Siberian iris). It has delicate leaves and flowers, which will tolerate a little shade or full sun and moist soils (photo 5). You'll find all shades of blue, purple, and white on 2-ft.- to 4-ft.-tall plants. Place Siberian iris in clumps in a few spots in the garden for early spring bloom, although it blooms later than bearded iris.

SHADE LOVERS

• I love the unusually variegated leaves of *Pulmonaria* 'Mrs. Moon'. Green leaves with white polka dots virtually glare in the low light and spread as a low-growing ground cover (8 in. tall by 12 in. to 16 in. wide) with creeping rootstocks. Small spring flowers in clusters above the leaves are reddish purple and funnel shaped, but grow this plant in full to partial shade for the spectacular leaves.

• *Hosta* ('Frances Williams') is a cultivar of *H. Sieboldiana* (photo 6). It has large, round leaves—10 in. to 15 in. across—with seersuckered texture, blue-green centers, and a creamy gold border. White flowers in midsummer shoot high in spikes above the leaves. The plant is formidable at 30 in. tall and 30 in. to 36 in. wide, so it's perfect to create a focal point in the garden. It's at home in shade or partial shade.

• I love the delicately scalloped light gray-green leaves of *Alchemilla mollis* (Lady's mantle), which form a 15-in. by 24-in. clump in the garden (photo 7). When it rains, a slight cupping of the leaves catches water, and the water beads on the lightly hairy surface. I'm not crazy about the short-lived, petalless, yellow flowers, but the habit and interesting foliage make a good texture foil for more showy plants in a partially shady garden.

(see the photo on p. 137). The downside is that you will be limited to compact varieties of plants.

I abandoned a fairly large vegetable garden in the country one season and planted potted tomatoes because I lacked the time to care for a large garden (I haven't grown tomatoes any other way since). A city dweller with little space need not abandon the love of gardening if there's a balcony available—there are many plant varieties suitable for container gardening. And a person with a bad back can continue working outside without all the bending needed to maintain a regular garden. The solution is to plant in containers that are raised to a suitable working height.

Whatever the reason for doing it, gardening in containers is one of the hottest trends in gardening.

When choosing containers, use your imagination. Don't feel as if you have to buy the typical pots from the garden center. A child's swimming pool, half whiskey barrels, trash barrels, window boxes, even old shoes will work. The most important concerns should be drainage, soil type, and watering. You should also think about whether overwintering in the containers will be a problem in your hardiness zone.

Drainage

Regardless of the container you choose, make sure you punch small holes in the bottom of it for drainage. Place a layer of stone or gravel at the bottom of the container or place a screen over the holes. The gravel or screen will retain the soil while allowing excess water to drain out.

Soil type

Use loam-based soil that's free of debris and weeds. If you are planting vegetables like tomatoes or pole beans that need support or climbing plants like morning glory, insert a cage or support when the plants are young to establish their upward movement.

Watering

Watering is a big issue with a container garden because the soil in a container dries out quickly—much faster than soil in a garden will. Unless you are willing to be a slave to watering the plants frequently, especially if you have sun-loving plants in the container, you may want to set up a drip-irrigation system on a timer.

Ready-made drip-irrigation kits are available at garden-supply houses, but you can make your own. Simply punch holes in a short length of plastic or rubber hose and plug, or cap, one end. Add a timer between the spigot and the hose, and the homemade system is ready for watering. Simply lay the hose on the soil in the containers. (If you opt for a drip-irrigation system, make sure the containers are near the water source. You don't want hoses lying all over the place.)

Overwintering

Overwintering in containers can be troublesome for people in cold climates. No matter how hard I tried in Vermont to grow perennials and shrubs in containers, it never worked. I tried covering the plants, mulching, and insulating the containers to no avail. So I experimented in other ways.

What finally worked was a large, raised planter box, which was also built 3 ft. below the ground. I also made sure that the plants were located at least 2 ft. in from the edges of the planter so that the roots would not contact the container, and I removed the bottom of the container to take advantage of the warmer ground below. Good snow cover was very important as an insulator.

Gardeners living in warmer hardiness zones, such as southern New England and west and south of there, should have no trouble with overwintering in containers, as long as the plants are well fertilized and watered.

Because of the growing trend in container gardening, most seed catalogs now offer several varieties of vegetables and flowers that stay compact and can be grown in containers, including peppers, cucumbers, tomatoes, and sunflowers. Annuals like marigolds, petunias, and geraniums have always been perfect window-box plants and so will thrive in other containers as well.

ROCK GARDENS

Although all of the gardens I've shown so far are beautiful, and some are even useful, the gardens I like most are rock gardens. I especially like the way plants wrap around the rocks and ramble through them.

The key to building an attractive rock garden is making it look natural in its setting by giving the garden an alpine feel. To get that feeling, it's best to create the garden on a slope and add alpine plantings.

As I discussed in Chapter 5, a rip-rap wall is an ideal method of retaining slope, but it's also a great opportunity to plant a rock garden amid the boulders. Doing so will allow the rip-rap wall to blend into the earth and the surrounding landscape. If you don't have a sloped area in your yard already, you can create a one-sided retaining wall, preferably out of stone, and backfill the other side (for more on building retaining walls, see Chapter 5). Then add rocks and boulders to the slope and plant around them.

When creating a rock garden, use rocks that look similar. Place them at infrequent intervals, buried partway into the ground and turned in the same direction. The result will be a natural-looking outcropping, similar to a native alpine site.

For planting between the rocks, choose alpine perennials, sun-loving small perennials, and dwarf conifers and shrubs (see the photo at right). These are small plants that will draw attention to the garden but will not hide the rocks.

I love the miniature features of alpine perennials and the way they sprawl over rocks. Alpines are native to high elevations and do not grow over 6 in. tall. Many spread with glee when given the space, and, unfortunately, may overtake less-invasive species. Some form cushionlike mounds, and others lie flat like mats. Flowers and leaves are delicate in texture and appearance, belying the toughness of plants able to withstand the open, harsh weather of rocky screes and crags. Some genera are so tiny that

Dwarf conifers stay in scale with low-growing rock-garden perennials.

PLANTS FOR ROCK GARDENS

• *Saponaria Ocymoides* (soapwort) is one of my favorite rock-garden plants because of its small, light-pink flowers profusely borne above tiny oval leaves on wiry stems (photo 1). It blooms in late spring, spreads to at least 18 in., and reaches 10 in. in height. It's a soft-colored alternative to the more common creeping phlox.

• Long, elliptical silver-leaved *Veronica incana* blooms on 8-in. amethyst-blue spikes in early summer and spreads over rocks as a low ground cover (photo 2).

• In contrast, light and airy *Gypsophila repens* (creeping baby's breath) trails over slopes and bears white or pink flowers in early summer.

• The daisylike blooms of *Chrysanthemum* 'Snow-cap' (dwarf Shasta), red and yellow *Gaillardia* 'Golden Goblin' (photo 3) and *G.* 'Baby Cole', and the yellow dwarf *Coreopsis* 'Goldfink'

contrast with one another. Each has flat flowers and a clumping habit.

• No rock garden is complete without the bellflowers, *Campanula carpatica*, *C. garganica*, and *C. muralis*, filling crevices and rocks with a long season of bloom in blue, white, and purple. The alpine *C. cochleariifolia* is a gem with pale blue or white bells in summer.

• An underused rock-garden candidate is *Oenothera missourensis* (Missouri primrose), with huge yellow flowers on stems 6 in. to 8 in. tall (photo 4). It blooms from early summer through frost. Allow enough space for it to sprawl, as one plant will spread 2 ft. to 3 ft. and maybe even more.

• *Sedum spurium, S. kamtschaticum,* and *S. brevifolium* (sedums) are the queens of the rock garden (photo 5). Their succulent foliage, sometimes tinged red or blue, and bright pink, yellow, or red flowers add brilliance to any site.

• I also like *Sempervivum arachnoideum* (photo 6) with white hairy webs covering red-tinged rosettes of fleshy leaves. It spreads everywhere, seemingly growing straight out of the rocks in the garden!

• Many dwarf shrubs provide the backdrop and framework of the rock garden and remain for winter interest after the alpines and perennials have faded. *Ilex crenata* 'Mariesii' is a broad-leaved evergreen holly with a low, mounded habit.

• A bright-green evergreen with tight, short, juvenile needles is *Juniperus procumbens* 'Nana' (Japanese garden juniper). It mounds and spreads very slowly.

• Upright dwarf conifers like *Juniperus communis* 'Compressa' and *Picea glauca* var. *albertiana* 'Conica' (dwarf Alberta spruce) contrast with all the ground-hugging plants.

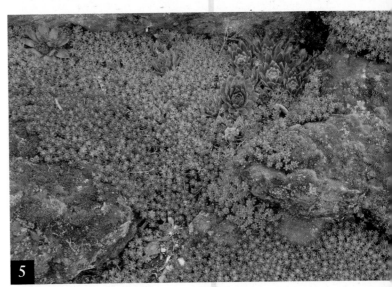

Alpines are well adapted to dry soils. When mixing them with small perennials or dwarf shrubs that prefer moist soil, make sure you plant the alpines in pockets of well-drained stony soil.

it is necessary to get on your hands and knees to appreciate their brilliant intricacy.

Perennials that stay within about 12 in. tall mix well with alpine perennials. And dwarf conifers and shrubs will also stay in scale with the small herbaceous alpines.

Because spacing is tight in a rock garden, it is especially important to lay out the plants before digging. This way you are sure the plants will fit and that you like the layout. Also, most alpines like dry, rocky

soil, which may be different than what some of the other plants in the garden like. So you have to make pockets of well-drained, stonier soils for the alpines and pockets of moisture-retaining soil for the other plant choices (see the photo above). Around the alpines, add a layer of small shards and rocks to allow the soil to drain and to keep leaves away from excess moisture, which could cause fungal diseases. To retain moisture for other plants, add mulch or make inconspicuous dams on the lower sides of the plants to catch water (a

list of plants suitable for a rock garden is given on pp. 142-143).

Finally, be sure to tuck your favorite ornaments into the rock garden in surprising venues to delight passersby (for more on garden ornamentation, see Chapter 8).

EDIBLE GARDENS

Many avid gardeners I know started out simply by growing herbs, vegetables, or fruit. Eventually, the satisfaction of growing their own food spawned a love for planting, which germinated into the desire to experiment with other types of gardens and garden projects. But just because an edible garden is utilitarian in nature, that doesn't mean it can't be an attractive part of the landscape plan. You can mix size, shape, texture, and color to create an edible feast for the eyes as well as for the palate.

There are three types of edible gardens—herb, vegetable, and fruit—but an edible garden can include all or some of these plants.

Herb gardens

Herb gardens are gaining in popularity. Any cook can attest to the fact that there's nothing better for a dish than freshly picked herbs from the yard (see the photo below).

An herb garden can simply sprout in a small plot or container or be as fancy as the knot gardens of England, with brick paths, sculpture, and low-manicured boxwood hedging enclosing the herbs. Aside from its size, the most-important consideration in creating an herb garden is that it be located for easy access from the kitchen, so a quick snip for soup, salad, or any other dish is easy.

An herb garden will not only season your favorite dishes, but it will also season the yard. Plan it as an ornamental treat, with low-maintenance, sun-loving plants. Some good choices, both annual and perennial, include sage (*Salvia officinalis*) with gray-green leaves and spikes of lavender flowers; purple basil (*Ocimum* 'Dark Opal')

Herbs like sweet woodruff, French tarragon, catmint, and lavender make a simple herb garden.

FRAGRANT PLANTS

This list is only a fraction of the plants available for a fragrant garden, and I certainly would include the old standbys of lilac and rose, but half the fun of gardening is discovering new plants on your own. Aromatic foliage usually needs to be crushed to release its fragrance.

GROUND COVERS

• Try *Rhus aromatica* (fragrant sumac*)*, which is a great ground-cover plant, *Perovskia* (Russian sage*)*, a large perennial with blue flowers (photo 1), and any of the thymes. I use thyme between cracks in a patio or walkway where light foot traffic will send its scent upward. Don't forget *Lavendula* (lavender), which makes a perfect edging plant for the front of a perennial garden. Its contrasting gray leaves look great all season long.

VINES

• The granddaddy of all fragrant vines is *Wisteria*, with purple or white flowers, but it needs strong support.

• *Lathyrus odoratus* (sweet peas) should be planted near a doorway or window so the scent can waft into the house.

• *Clematis* (*C. Armandii* and *C. montana*) (photo 2) and *Lonicera* (honey-suckle) grow well on sunny walls in cooler climates.

• *Beaumontia grandiflora* (herald's trumpet) and *Stephanotis floribunda* (jasmine) (photo 3) do best in warm climates. Jasmine's scent is strongest at night, making it the perfect candidate for wowing your guests at a summer's evening barbecue.

SHRUBS

• One of my favorite fragrant shrubs is *Daphne*, especially 'Carol Mackie' with variegated green and white leaves. It grows to a 4-ft. mound and blooms in early spring with light-pink flowers (see photo 6 on p. 131).

• *Hamamelis* (witch hazel), *Philadelphus* (mock orange), and *Buddleia Davidii* (butterfly bush) are found in old-fashioned gardens.

Witch hazel can become large, so try the smallest one, *H. vernalis,* growing to 10 ft. and blooming in winter. Mock orange grows to about 6 ft. or more and really smells like oranges when it blooms in the spring. Butterfly bush grows 6 ft. to 10 ft. tall and has long clusters of white or pink flowers from summer to fall. Try *B.* 'Black Knight' for wine-red blossoms.

• *Viburnum Carlesii* (Korean spice viburnum) will add fragrance to and enhance a garden in light shade. It grows to 5 ft. and has white flower clusters in spring.

• There are also several fragrant *Rhododendrons* (*R. luteum, R. occidentale, R. viscosum*), which will do best in a woodland situation. These natives all grace a wild garden in spring with white or pink blossoms. All can reach as high as 8 ft. to 10 ft. but will stay smaller in cultivation.

• For southern climates, *Gardenias* are absolutely intoxicating. They bloom from spring to fall and prefer acidic soil. They can reach 2 ft. to 5 ft. tall and their glossy, dark-green foliage contrasts the creamy white blossoms beautifully.

TREES

• Everyone is familiar with the scented flowers of trees like magnolias, cherries, and crab apples, but how many have appreciated the scent of *Tilia* (linden)? The flowers are really nothing to look at, and they hide under the leaves, but for about two weeks in early summer, there isn't a spicier fragrance in the air.

• Tropical gardeners will love *Plumeria obtusa* (frangipani) (photo 4) and *Acacia dealbata,* which offers winter perfume.

3

4

BED SYSTEM OF PLANTING VEGETABLES

Planting small vegetable beds with paths between allows easy access to all sides of the beds for cultivation. It also creates an opportunity to mix colors and textures to make an eye-pleasing design.

KEY TO BEDS

A. Bell peppers and hot peppers
B. Iceburg lettuce and corn
C. Carrots and spinach
D. Tomatoes and marigolds
E. Leaf lettuce
F. Onions with zucchini in the trellis

for showy leaves and pink flowers (although the green-leaved *O. Basilicum* 'Minimum' is more tasty for pesto); and lemon thyme (*Thymus × citriodorus* 'Doone Valley'), a sprawler with fruity fragrance and small green leaves, marbled with white, yellow, and red. The old standbys of dill, rosemary, parsley, oregano, and chives can be included, and they won't disappoint you in texture, foliage, or flowers.

Vegetable gardens

A vegetable garden can be the focus of the landscape or it can simply blend into it. In either case, some general planting guidelines apply.

A vegetable garden should be located in a sunny, open portion of the yard, away from shady areas such as trees or buildings. Staying away from leaf-dropping trees is also important because old leaves can harbor diseases and, as they break down or compost, will rob valuable nitrogen from the soil and lower the pH.

The site should not be exposed to a lot of wind. Too much wind will cause lower yields because pollination will be sparse and irregular. If you have a lot of wind, plant a windbreak or erect a fence to lessen its force. But you don't want a solid barrier against the wind. A windbreak or fence around a vegetable garden should be permeable enough to allow gentle breezes through. Otherwise, the wind will tunnel over or around them, increasing its force within the garden.

Once you have settled on a location, you must carefully consider the layout of the garden.

Traditionally, vegetables have been grown in rows with taller crops like corn at one end and squashes and cucumbers in raised mounds. A newer trend is to plant crops in beds narrow enough to reach from all sides, with small paths surrounding the beds (see the drawing on the facing page). The paths can be bricked, mulched with bark, or even left as grass as long as they are not too small for the mower.

Creating smaller beds makes watering, fertilizing, and crop rotation easier. The beds can be round, square, rectangular, or any shape that is narrow enough to be easily accessible. (By accessible I mean being able to reach all the plants within a bed without walking into it.)

Plants should be spaced equally, and single crops of two or more compatible types can be interplanted for even more efficiency and interest. For instance, fast-growing crops like radishes can be interplanted with slow-growing parsnips. The radishes can be harvested before the parsnips will need the extra room to mature. Lettuces benefit from the shade of slower, taller corn and will be harvested before the corn matures. Interplanting also allows you to mix size, color, shape, and texture to create a pleasing design.

An added bonus of interplanting is that you can grow plants that may help keep pests away from the crop. For instance, planting pungent herbs like garlic and mint with tomatoes will discourage pests that are attracted by smell. The plant doesn't necessarily have to be

edible, either: Marigolds make a fine skirt of color around the bottom of a single tomato plant, and they attract hoverflies, which feed on aphids.

If there is not a lot of room to plant a vegetable garden, you can make the most of the space available by utilizing trellises, poles, or archways to provide support for crops like scarlet runner beans, peas, squash, and cucumbers. The dangling vegetables are very ornamental and easy to harvest because you don't have to bend over.

For very small spaces, vegetables can be grown in containers as long as they are planted in well-drained light soils and located in sheltered, sunny spots close to a water source. The larger the container, the better, especially for heavy feeders like tomatoes and potatoes. Set up a drip-irrigation system (available at garden-supply houses, or you can make your own), so you will not have to be a slave to watering. Use supports like cages and bamboo canes to support heavily foliaged plants and vines.

Quick-harvested crops like radishes, lettuce, and beets are ideal for container growing, as well as peppers, eggplants, and leafy vegetables like Swiss chard. Dwarf cultivars of many popular varieties are available.

You should avoid growing deep-rooting crops such as broccoli or celery in containers because they need more space than is available in a container.

Espaliered fruit trees save space when your yard is small and can also dress up a boring fence.

Fruit or nut gardens

It is always a bonus to plant for ornamental purposes and to receive a bounty of fruit or nuts at the same time. Whether you garden on a balcony in the city or in an expansive, rural yard, a harvest can be yours to enjoy.

What makes fruit- and nut-bearing trees and shrubs so appealing to me is that they can be relegated to their own spot in the yard or mixed with other plants to add interest to the landscape. Blueberries, for instance,

with striking red fall color, make a fine ornamental shrub.

When planting fruit trees or shrubs, choose a site that is permanent and easy to maintain because good production requires special care. It is wise to group together plants with similar needs to make it easier to apply fertilizer or to protect them from animals, birds, and wind. It is also important to remember that some fruit crops (apples, pears, and sweet cherries, for instance) must be sited near pollinators to produce fruit. (You'll

need to research your plant choices carefully to find out their needs and whether or not they are compatible with other plants in the bed.)

If you have a small yard, you can still grow fruit trees and shrubs. Many trees are grafted on dwarf rootstocks, which will keep the plants small and in scale with the space. Another option is to espalier fruit trees or shrubs to a fence or lattice (see the photo above). Vines like grapes or kiwis can be supported by trellises and archways, and strawberries and figs can be planted in containers as long as ample water and fertilizer are at hand (see the photo below).

Most *Citrus* species are suitable for small areas. They are self-fertile and bloom during any season in subtropical climates as long as it is warm (58°F to 86°F), humid (60% to 70%), and rainfall is ample. Lemons and limes make particularly good container crops for the small-space garden (see the photo on p. 152), but they'll need a sunny, sheltered site and well-drained, slightly acidic soil.

Citrus trees can be grown in cool, temperate climates during the warm months, but the lower light and cooler temperatures may hamper fruit production, although the evergreen aromatic leaves will remain very ornamental. Citrus can be brought indoors for the winter

A fine crop of strawberries is possible in containers as long as there is ample water and nourishment.

Citrus trees need sunny sites sheltered from the wind. If planted in a container, the tree can be brought indoors for winter.

to a sunroom or greenhouse where the temperature and humidity requirements can be maintained.

Aside from the usual fruit-bearing variety of trees, such as apple, for sunny, open yards, there are many nut-bearing trees that can add interest to the landscape. In large, temperate sites, a pecan tree (*Carya illinoinensis*) can make a majestic specimen for the backyard, and, in cooler climates, chestnuts (*Castanea*) (see the photo on the facing page) and walnuts (*Juglans regia*) will substitute nicely.

Almonds (*Prunus dulcis*) are small trees for warm sites, reaching only 15 ft. to 20 ft. tall, although they can be pruned to accommodate a

Chestnut (*Castanea*) is a cool-weather, nut-bearing tree for a sunny, open yard.

smaller space. Hazelnuts (*Corylus Avellana*) and filberts (*C. maxima*) like partially shaded, protected locations. They have spreads of 12 ft. to 15 ft. but can be pruned to stay smaller. All are wind pollinated and self-fertile except for almonds, which are insect pollinated and sometimes only partially self-fertile (depending on the cultivar). Those cultivars will be more productive if another pollinating cultivar is planted nearby.

GARDENING WITH BULBS

For me, there's no better way to signal the end of winter and the start of the growing season than with early blooming bulbs. And there is nothing more evocative of the freshness of the season, nor more filled with the anticipation of summer, than a huge bouquet of daffodils or tulips on the dining-room table.

My woodland garden in Vermont has a spectacular spring display of *Crocus* and *Narcissus* (daffodil) (photo 1). Before the leaves unfurl on the trees, the *Crocus* in the foreground bloom in shades of white, purple, and yellow. As their show ends, the daffodil show begins. I have double yellow and orange ('Tahiti'), double white and yellow ('Cheerfulness'), white with yellow-orange cups ('Pride of Cornwall'), all yellow ('King Alfred'), all white ('Mount Hood'), yellow with orange cups ('Ambergate'), and creamy whites with just a blush of salmon-pink ('Passionale'). I love the masses of color beneath the trees that herald the start of the growing season.

My favorite tulips for early spring are the botanical tulips like 'Red Riding Hood' (photo 2), a brilliant red that only reaches 6 in. to 8 in. in height and has maroon-striped, green leaves. Spotted around my rock garden, they make flashes of color in concert with *Muscari* (grape hyacinth), *Galanthus* (white snowdrops), and *Narcissus* 'Tête-à-tête' (dwarf daffodil).

Don't discount all-white tulips, which, in a large mass, evoke quite a feeling of elegance and simplicity. I also plant groups of white tulips in between other colors to buffer strong, warm reds and yellows. There are early-, midseason-, and late-blooming tulips in all colors for a continuous spring spectacle.

I am very fond of planting bulbs of the same species or cultivars together in a group to make sizable spots of interest. But to provide successive color in a garden, plant six or eight tulips or daffodils in a cluster near perennials that bloom later, covering the remnants of the bulbs.

I like to plant *Allium* (photo 3) in all sizes. The most imposing, *A. giganteum,* have huge, 8-in. balls of purple flowers on 2-ft. stalks. The midsize *A. aflatunense* is my favorite, with purple flower heads that are 4 in. across. They bloom at the same time as my pink poppies, and then I leave the round, curious-looking seed heads as whimsical companions for the iris and delphinium seasons.

PLANTING GUIDELINES

You can start planting bulbs for spring color in late summer into the late autumn. No matter what size bulb you plant, a few general guidelines apply.

Plant bulbs about three to five times their own depth and about two to three bulb widths apart. The easiest way to plant a number of them is to dig one long hole at the correct depth for the bulb type you are planting and place several in the hole the correct distance apart. Make sure the root end is pointing down.

Sprinkle the ground with a bulb starter, such as bone meal, phosphorus, or commercial bulb booster, and then cover the bulbs with soil. Tamp firmly to eliminate any air pockets.

Water thoroughly and deeply, continuing on occasion until winter sets in. Then sit back and wait until spring.

3

CHAPTER 12

Hiring a Landscape Architect, Designer, or Contractor

For some readers, a number of the projects and techniques in this book are beyond their skill level, so they need the help of a professional. If this applies to you, the information in this book will help you become a first-rate consumer when it comes to hiring a professional to design or build the landscape or features within it.

But with so many architects, designers, and contractors out there, how do you choose one? Here are some general guidelines that, when combined with the information in this book, will help you make an educated decision. Be sure the person you hire has a license if required, that you have seen and like the work he does, that he has good references, and that the costs to do the job will not exceed your budget.

LICENSING REQUIREMENTS

Become familiar with your state's laws regarding professional landscape architects, designers, and contractors. If you are looking for a professional designer or architect (although many landscape contractors are designers as well), keep in mind that these titles could mean different things in different states.

Just because a person says he is an architect or designer, don't automatically think that he has a license or even formal training.

In general, the differences between a landscape designer and a landscape architect are the number of years of graduate study, the depth or scope of the work performed, and certainly the price tag for that work (an architect will typically charge more).

But just because a person says he is an architect or designer, don't automatically think that he has a license or even formal training. License requirements and laws vary from state to state. For instance, in Vermont, anyone can call himself a landscape architect, regardless of training and ability. In other states, like Massachusetts and California, there are very strict requirements for licensing akin to those of engineers and architects.

But in my opinion, neither a license from the state nor accreditation from a school provides a clear indication of the breadth of knowledge an architect or designer might possess. For instance, I have known landscape architects who drew exquisite plans and made great models of landscapes, but they didn't know the difference between a sugar maple and an ash tree. By the same token, there are great landscape designers out there who have only a cursory knowledge of contours but who design superb gardens.

Some states require landscape contractors to be licensed. But, unfortunately, there are many states in which anyone can buy a pickup truck and a shovel and start a landscape business. Many of these fly-by-nighters will be out of business next year, and any guarantees that were promised you will be gone too. So, when hiring an independent contractor, do some research.

THE SEARCH

One of the easiest ways to find an architect, designer, or contractor is to drive around and look for landscapes you like. When you come across one, find out who designed and installed it. If friends or neighbors had some work done that you like, ask them for the name of the contractor and designer.

Some states require landscape contractors to be licensed. But there are many states in which anyone can buy a pickup truck and a shovel and start a landscape business. Many of these fly-by-nighters will be out of business next year, and any guarantees that were promised you will be gone too.

If this doesn't work for you, use the yellow pages or ask people at the local garden center to name a few architects, designers, or contractors.

Another option is to consult with members of the local chapters of associations related to landscaping, such as the Association of Professional Landscape Designers (APLD), the American Society of Landscape Architects (ASLA), or Allied Landscape Contractors of America (ALCA). To get into one of these associations, an architect, designer, or contractor may have to submit samples of his work to a jury and must constantly reeducate himself to remain a member. So the names you get should be credible.

WORK EXAMPLES AND REFERENCES

Pare the list down to three names. Because choosing a professional landscape architect, designer, or contractor is not something you can, or should, do without seeing his work, arrange to see examples (if you have not seen any yet), either from a portfolio or in real life.

Ask for references. Get the name and phone number of the owners of the landscapes you've seen pictured and liked. Pick jobs that have been in place for at least five years, so you know they have held up over time. You will be making a huge investment in time and money that will affect the value of your home by as much as 15% to 20%. If the architect, designer, or contractor will not provide references, look elsewhere.

Ask the previous clients general questions not only about the work but also about whether the architect, designer, or contractor met deadlines and was flexible. Deadlines are important, especially if you are paying by the hour.

There should be no surprises. If your goal is to get a front walk and six plants, that's exactly what you should get.

By flexibility, I mean ego—just that. Is the person willing to work with you? Will he meet your needs and listen to you and not just forge ahead with a design just because he thinks it's right? I've had many clients tell me horror stories about paying for useless plans, where the architect clearly did not ask the right questions or give the home-owner the opportunity for input during the planning process. If the person you hire is not on the right track, it is your right to communicate with him to try to correct it.

BUDGET

The last consideration is monetary. It's important that the architect, designer, or contractor work within your budget and deliver what you ask for. There should be no surprises. If your goal is to get a front walk and six plants, that's exactly what you should get.

If it seems as if the costs are exceeding what you originally planned for, or if the architect, designer, or contractor has an idea that will add to the budget—and you like it—the person should work with you to alter the design to fit

When a working plan has been completed, both designer and homeowner should go out in the yard and discuss it to see how things will work.

that idea into the budget. He may ask to eliminate an item or two from the plan to bring costs down, or he may suggest phasing in the project over a period of time so that you stay within your budget.

You should be able to communicate your needs and desires, and the architect, designer, or contractor should be given the freedom to employ his or her creative abilities.

In general, landscape architects, designers, and contractors don't come cheap, and this is truly a business where you get what you pay for. When you have a few bids, throw out the lowest one just on principle. Then spend an ample amount of time comparing the highest bid with the middle one, looking for what is and what is not included in the price, what is guaranteed, and what materials will be used and whether they will cost extra. The best value might not be the lowest priced, and it may be well worth your while to pay the extra buck.

Sometimes, the contractor may be the designer also, performing the function of a design-build firm. This is not a bad route to go because you could save some money. Often the installation offers the contractor the higher profit margin, so he may discount doing the plans just so he gets the installation.

WORKING RELATIONSHIP

Once you have chosen a landscape architect, designer, or contractor, it's time to go to work. Remember, he is working for you, and you should be involved throughout the process. But the job is a give-and-take situation, a partnership; neither party should dictate to the other.

Maintain a constant dialogue throughout the design-and-build process. This should not be an adversarial relationship. You should be able to communicate your needs and desires, and the architect, designer, or contractor should be given the freedom to employ his or her creative abilities to best illustrate your desires on paper or in the ground. Remember, you have hired a professional for his expertise. If you dictate what you want without regard to his advice and knowledge, with him simply regurgitating your ideas, why did you bother hiring him in the first place? You have to give a certain amount of latitude and trust to the person you hire.

When a working plan is presented to you, you should expect a full explanation. Both designer and homeowner should go out in the yard and lay the design out with props if need be. At this time, because the plan is still malleable, it can be changed. If you don't like something, say so, and if the designer has suggestions, listen to him—don't be adverse to suggestions yourself.

The architect, designer, or contractor should also show you pictures or may even ask that you visit the garden center (or some previous jobs) together to look at the plants and materials he has suggested. This is a valuable exercise because the plants that actually are installed in your yard will probably be smaller and may not be in bloom. Take the time to look at the plants with the designer so you will be familiar with them when they mature.

In general, landscape architects, designers, and contractors don't come cheap. Spend time comparing the highest bid with the middle one, looking for what is and what is not included in the price, what is guaranteed, and what materials will be used and whether they will cost extra. The best value might not be the lowest priced, and it may be well worth your while to pay the extra buck.

A good working relationship with the architect, designer, or contractor will be well worth the patience and cooperation you both demonstrate. If you had a good relationship, and for some reason a plant dies or a concept doesn't work, the professional will be more apt to correct the problem in a timely, friendly fashion.

USDA Plant-Hardiness Zone Map

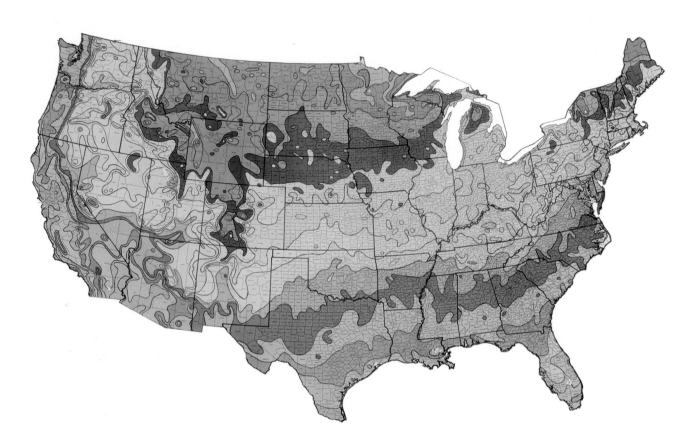

Average Annual Minimum Temperature by Zone	
Zone	**Temperature °F**
1	below -50
2a	-45 to -50
2b	-40 to -45
3a	-35 to -40
3b	-30 to -35
4a	-25 to -30
4b	-20 to -25
5a	-15 to -20
5b	-10 to -15
6a	-5 to -10
6b	0 to -5
7a	5 to 0
7b	10 to 5
8a	15 to 10
8b	20 to 15
9a	25 to 20
9b	30 to 25
10a	35 to 30
10b	40 to 35
11	40 and above

This map shows the United States divided into 11 zones. To use the map, simply find the zone where you live and choose plants designated to grow well in your zone. Be aware, however, that other factors, including soil, exposure, moisture, and drainage, affect the growth of plants.

Further Reading

Andersen Source List, 4th edition. Horticultural Library, University of Minnesota. Minnesota Landscape Arboretum. Chanhassen, Minnesota. (List of retail and wholesale nurseries indexed by plant name.)

Arnoux, Jean-Claude. *The Ultimate Water Garden Book*. Newtown, Connecticut: The Taunton Press, Inc., 1996.

Carley, Rachel. *The Backyard Book*. Edited by Tricia Foley. New York: Viking Penguin, Inc., 1988.

Chatto, Beth. *The Green Tapestry*. New York: Simon and Schuster, 1989.

Dirr, Michael A. *The Manual of Woody Landscape Plants*. Champaign, Illinois: Stipes Publishing Co., 1990.

Druse, Ken. *The Natural Garden*. New York: Crown Publishing Group, 1988.

Fischer, Kerwin. *Green Places in Small Spaces*. Newtown, Connecticut: The Taunton Press, Inc., 1997.

Fisher, Sue. *The Hanging Garden*. North Pomfret, Vermont: Trafalgar Square, 1996.

Gershuny, Grace, and Deborah Martin, eds. *The Rodale Book of Composting*. Emmaus, Pennsylvania: Rodale Press, 1992.

Greenlee, John. *The Encyclopedia of Ornamental Grasses*. Emmaus, Pennsylvania: Rodale Press, 1992.

Joyce, David, and Susan Conder. *Variegated Leaves*. Old Tappan, New Jersey: MacMillan, 1994.

Lacey, Stephen. *Scent in Your Garden*. New York: Little, Brown, and Co., 1991.

Olkowski, William, Sheila Daar, and Helga Olkowski. *The Gardener's Guide to Common-Sense Pest Control*. Newtown, Connecticut: The Taunton Press, Inc., 1996.

Pavord, Anna. *The New Kitchen Garden*. New York: DK Publishing, 1996.

Schuttner, Scott. *Building and Designing Decks*. Newtown, Connecticut: The Taunton Press, Inc., 1993.

Search, Gay. *Gardening Without a Garden*. New York: DK Publishing, 1997.

Stadelman, Peter. *Water Gardens*. Hauppauge, New York: Barron's Educational Series, Inc., 1992.

van Sweden, James. *Gardening with Water*. New York: Random House, 1995.

von Trapp, Sara Jane. *Landscape Doctor*. Shelburne, Vermont: Chapters Publishing, 1994.

Woods, Chris. *Encyclopedia of Perennials*. New York: Facts on File, 1996.

Sources

Plants, bulbs, and seeds

Breck's
6523 N. Galena Road
P.O. Box 1757
Peoria, IL 61656-1757
(800) 722-9069
Mail-order flower bulbs.

Dutch Gardens, Inc.
P.O. Box 200
Adelphia, NJ 07710
(800) 818-3861
Mail-order flower bulbs
from Holland.

Charles Klehm & Sons Nursery
4210 N. Duncan Road
Champaign, IL 61821
(800) 553-3715
Mail-order perennials, including
daylilies, hostas, peonies, and
some woody plants.

Lilypons Water Gardens
P.O. Box 10, Dept. 2426
Buckeystown, MD 21717-0010
(800) 723-7667
Mail-order water plants
and supplies.

Milaeger's Gardens
4838 Douglas Ave.
Racine, WI 53402-2498
(800) 669-9956
Perennials, grasses, prairie
plants, vines, and bulbs.

Park Seed
1 Parkton Ave.
Greenwood, SC 29648-0046
(800) 222-3543
Mail-order seed catalogs.

Van Bourgondien Bros.
Box 1000
Babylon, NY 11702
(800) 552-9996
Mail-order bulbs.

Wayside Gardens Co.
Hodges, SC 29695
(800) 845-1124
Mail-order seeds.

Garden equipment and supplies

The Clapper Co.
1121 Washington St.
West Newton, MA 02165
(617) 244-7900
Mail-order tools, garden furniture,
garden ornaments, and other
garden equipment.

Drip-Rite Irrigation Products
3315 Monier Circle, Suite 2
Rancho Cordova, CA 95742
(916) 635-7401
e-mail: DripIrr@aol.com
Drip-irrigation products
and equipment.

Green Gems
P.O. Box 6007
Healdsburg, CA 95448-6007
(800) 431-SOIL
Mail-order soil-testing kits.

Robert Compton Pottery
3600 Route 116
Bristol, VT 05443
(802) 453-3778
Ready-to-plug-in stoneware
fountains for indoor or out.

Country Home Products, Inc.
Meigs Road, P.O. Box 25
Vergennes, VT 05491
(800) 446-8746
Trimmers, mowers, brush cutters
with innovative designs.

Escort Lighting
201 Sweitzer Road
Sinking Spring, PA 19608
(800) 856-7948
Finely crafted garden lighting
in solid copper.

Gardener's Supply Co.
128 Intervale Road
Burlington, VT 05401
(800) 315-4005
Garden tools and equipment and
organic fertilizers and pesticides.

Lee Valley Tools, Ltd.
12 East River St.
Ogdensburg, NY 13669
(800) 871-8158
Mail-order gardening tools
and accessories.

Mantis Manufacturing Co.
1028 Street Road
Southampton, PA 18966
(800) 366-6268
Lightweight garden tillers.

Nitron Industries, Inc.
P.O. Box 1447
Fayetteville, AR 72707
(800) 835-0123
Organic growing supplies.

Resource Conservation
Technology, Inc.
2633 N. Calvert St.
Baltimore, MD 21218
(410) 366-1146
Rubber liners for garden ponds.

Tetra Pond
3001 Commerce St.
Blacksburg, VA 24060
(540) 951-5400
Water-garden equipment
and supplies.

Troy-Bilt
1 Garden Way
Troy, NY 12180
(800) 446-4991
A wide range of garden tillers.

Wicker Warehouse
195 South River St.
Hackensack, NJ 07601
(800) 989-4253
Discounted garden furniture.

Garden structures

City Visions, Inc.
311 Seymour St.
Lansing, MI 48933
(517) 372-3385
Outdoor structures.

Gardensheds
651 Millcross Road
Lancaster, PA 17601
(717) 397-5430
Potting sheds, storage buildings,
and wood containers.

Kinsman Co., Inc.
River Road
Point Pleasant, PA 18950
(800) 733-4146
Compost bins, strawberry tubs,
and modular arbors, as well as
English garden tools.

Fences

Delgard Premier
Aluminum Fencing
8600 River Road
Delair, NJ 08110
(800) 235-0185
Aluminum fencing.

Saratoga Rail Fence & Supply, Inc.
P.O. Box 13864
Albany, NY 12212-9600
(800) 869-8703
PVC fencing.

Retaining-wall and patio systems

Keystone Retaining Walls
4444 West 78th St.
Minneapolis, MN 55435
(612) 897-1040
Retaining-wall systems.

Pave Tech, Inc.
P.O. Box 31126
Bloomington, MN 55431
(800) 728-3832
Underground black PVC edging
for concrete pavers and bricks.

Risi Stone Systems
8500 Leslie St., Suite 390
Thornhill, L3T 7P1, Ont., Canada
(905) 882-5898
Concrete wall systems.

Uni Paving Group USA
4362 Northlake Blvd., Suite 207
Palm Beach Gardens, FL 33410
(407) 626-4666
Concrete pavers and supply
info about local dealers.

Photo Credits

Chapter 1
p. 4, Ken Druse
pgs. 7, 13, Kathleen Kolb
p. 8, Susan Kahn
p. 9, Sloan Howard

Chapter 2
p. 17, Sloan Howard
p. 20 left, Derek Fell
p. 20 right, Pamela Harper
p. 24, Scott Phillips

Chapter 3
pgs. 25, 30, Susan Kahn
p. 29 top, Kathleen Kolb
pgs. 29 bottom, 31, Alan Detrick
p. 32, Scott Phillips

Chapter 4
pgs. 34, 40, 41, Scott Phillips
p. 37, Susan Kahn
p. 38, Kathleen Kolb
p. 39, Pamela Harper

Chapter 5
pgs. 45, 46, Derek Fell
pgs. 48, 52, 54, 58, 59, Kathleen Kolb
p. 51, Alden Pellett
p. 53 top and bottom left, Keystone
    Retaining Walls
p. 53 right, Risi Stone Systems

Chapter 6
pgs. 60, 61, 62, 63 bottom, 64, 65,
    Kathleen Kolb
p. 63 top, *Fine Gardening* staff
p. 66, Alan Detrick
pgs. 68, 73, Alden Pellet
pgs. 69, 70 bottom, 71, 72, Susan Kahn
p. 70 top, Sloan Howard
pgs. 74 left, 75 top, California Redwood
    Association
pgs. 74 right, 75 bottom, Charles Miller

Chapter 7
pgs. 76, 77, 78 left, 79, 80 bottom,
    Courtesy of Walpole Woodworkers
p. 78 right, Ken Druse
pgs. 80 top, 84, 89 bottom, Kathleen
    Kolb
pgs. 82 top left, middle left, middle
    right, 83 top left, middle left, 89
    top, 92 top, 94 bottom, Pamela
    Harper
pgs. 82 bottom left, 83 bottom left,
    middle right, bottom right, 93, 94
    top, 95, Derek Fell
pgs. 82 top right, bottom right, 83 top
    right, Charles Mann
p. 86, Sloan Howard
p. 92 bottom, Karin O'Connor

Chapter 8
pgs. 96, 103, 105 bottom right, 107
    middle right, Pamela Harper
pgs. 97, 107 bottom right, Ken Druse
pgs. 98, 101, 105 top right, Derek Fell
pgs. 104 top and bottom, 105, 106
    bottom, Alan Detrick
p. 106 top, Sloan Howard
p. 107 left, Janet Loughrey
p. 107 top right, Author

Chapter 9
p. 110, Ken Druse
pgs. 111, 113, 115, 116, 117, 118,
    Sloan Howard
p. 112, Scott Phillips

Chapter 10
pgs. 117, 120, 121 bottom left, 122,
    Ken Druse
pgs. 118 top left, bottom right, 131
    middle right, Susan Roth
pgs. 118 middle left, 119 bottom, 121
    top left, middle left, 123 right, 127,
    131 top left, Derek Fell
pgs. 118 bottom left, 131 bottom right,
    Charles Mann
pgs. 118 top right, 121 bottom right,
    Alan Detrick
pgs. 119 top, middle, 121 top right,
    middle right, 123 top left, middle
    left, bottom left, 130 middle left,
    bottom left, bottom right, 131 top
    right, Pamela Harper
p. 130 top left, Susan Kahn

Chapter 11
pgs. 135, 154 top, Ken Druse
pgs. 136, 137, 138 middle left, bottom
    left, 143 top, 150, 151, 152, 153,
    155, Derek Fell
pgs. 138 top left, 143 bottom, 146
    bottom, Alan Detrick
pgs. 138 top right, 139 top and bottom,
    142 bottom left and right, 144,
    145, 146, 147 top and bottom,
    154, Pamela Harper
pgs. 138 bottom right, 142 top left,
    Charles Mann
p. 141, Susan Roth
p. 143 middle, Janet Loughrey

Chapter 12
p. 156, Sloan Howard
p. 158, Susan Kahn

Index

Associate publisher: Helen Albert
Editorial assistant: Cherilyn DeVries

Editor: Thomas McKenna
Designer/Layout artist: Lynne Phillips
Illustrator: Pat Schories
Indexer: Carolyn Mandarano

Typeface: Sabon/Giltus
Paper: 80-lb. Somerset Gloss
Printer: R.R. Donnelley and Sons Company, Willard, Ohio